Celebrity Past-Life Clues

Celebrity Past-Life Clues

A Closer Look Into the Past
Lives of 50 Famous People

Barbara Lane Ph.D.

Copyright © 2015

Authored By Barbara Lane Ph.D.

ISBN: 1508663610
ISBN 13: 9781508663614

Dedication

This book is dedicated to my loving and supportive family and friends; to the accomplished actors, actresses, and performers who are living out their souls' destinies as the shining lights that they are; and to all of you who are willing to unlock your potential as you sojourn through this mysterious life. May you all add your star to life's walk of fame.

With a grateful heart, I thank Dawn Janke for her professional editing skills, Cathy Merchand for her artistic cover creation, and everyone who inspires me.

Table of Contents

Preface

* * *

The Continuing Integration of Science, Consciousness, Time, and Reincarnation

What is consciousness? What happens to us after we die? Have we lived before?

After a mind-expanding experience of "universal consciousness" as he returned to earth from his moon walk more than forty years ago, former astronaut and scientist Edgar Mitchell, became convinced that the unchartered territory of the human mind was the next frontier to explore.[1]

As a metaphysician, exploring the unchartered territory of the human mind meant that scientific thinking might be merging with the theory of reincarnation and the possibility that regenerating our energy might be interpreted as the rebirth of the soul. I was delighted to see that scientific thinking was expanding its understanding of consciousness, especially because that opened space for the theory of reincarnation. Actually, if I had understood quantum physics back then, I would have realized that scientists indeed long had been exploring cosmology and consciousness from fresh perspectives.

While for me, Mitchell's expanded study of consciousness was eye-opening, the space-time continuum had been explored years prior to Mitchell's life-altering experience. As early as 1905, Albert Einstein examined the relationship between space and time and later declared "energy cannot be created or destroyed, it can only be changed from one form to another."[2] To my mind, this sounds like science-speak for the classic definition of reincarnation: the rebirth of the soul through lifetimes in human form.

Einstein believed that the distinction between the past, present, and future is only a stubbornly persistent illusion. "In truth," he said, "your mind transcends time and space."[3] Indeed, if, as many scientists believe, reality cannot exist without consciousness, then space and time can't either.

Modern-day scientists have carried these theories of space, time, and consciousness even further.

Well-known physicist Stephen Hawking is a vigorous supporter of the many-worlds interpretation of quantum mechanics. He believes that according to quantum physics, the past and the future are indefinite and exist only as a spectrum of possibilities."[4]

What's more, Dr. Robert Lanza, currently touted as the standard bearer for stem cell research and a proponent of biocentrism, says that, "scientific experiments suggest life is not a one-time deal."[5]

Lanza goes on to explain, "Biocentrism suggests that life is a flowering and adventure that transcends our ordinary linear way of thinking. Although our individual bodies are destined to self-destruct, the "me" feeling is just energy operating in the brain. But this energy doesn't go away at death."[6] Agreeing with the rule of conservation of energy, Lanza claims that "life has a non-linear dimensionality—it's like a perennial flower that returns to bloom in the multiverse."[7]

While Lanza explores biocentrism and the rule of conservation of energy, scientist Rupert Sheldrake focuses on morphic resonance, which points to the possibility that memory outlives the brain; such a theory offers a potential foundation for explaining reincarnation.

Sheldrake has challenged the notion that consciousness can be considered separately from the brain. His morphogenetic energy field theory, which seems to encompass racial memory and the collective unconscious, builds on pooled memory of similar species, a basis for claims of reincarnation.

Sheldrake postulates that we attract that to which we most resonate, which may in fact be our own past states, in his essay, "Can Our Memories Survive the Death of Our Brains?" Through the morphogenetic energy field, Sheldrake theorizes that the conscious self could retain the ability to tune in to its own past states, even after the death of the brain.[8]

Sheldrake's work is similar to that of spiritual guru Deepak Chopra's concept of a "network of intelligence," which is grounded in quantum physics. Early in his career, Chopra was an endrocrinologist, and at that time he wrote *Quantum Healing*, in which Chopra said, "A cell's memory is able to outlive itself . . . Your body is just a place your memory calls home."[9]

Concurrent with scientists examining and re-examining theories of space, time, consciousness, and reincarnation, psychologists have been studying cases of children who have recalled past lives and have come up with similar conclusions about its validity.

Dr. Jim Tucker of the University of Virginia, who has continued the studies of Dr. Ian Stevenson related to past-life memories, agrees with Sheldrake's work. In fact, the pair has collected case studies of children around the world who have recalled past lives. They have found that on every continent today, except Antarctica, children's past-life memories are surfacing.[10]

The belief in rebirth has been interwoven into the fabric of religion and philosophy as well as science and psychology. All ancient peoples believed that death was not the end. Specifically, the ancient Sumerians, Egyptians, and Greeks all had resurrection myths. The belief in reincarnation also has long been accepted by Hindus and Buddhists and is becoming increasingly adopted by westerners. As well, belief is present in the Judaic practice of Kabbalah, which mentions reincarnation in numerous texts.[11]

But not all religious traditions embrace reincarnation. It is possible, for example, that more westerners would believe in the philosophy today if it hadn't been deemed politically incorrect by the Roman Catholic Church. Some historians look to the Council of Nicaea in 325 A.D. as the point at which the Emperor Constantine negotiated the condemnation of the doctrine. Others credit the Byzantine Emperor Justinian and his wife with obliterating most of the references to reincarnation from the Bible in the sixth century.

Neither all religions nor all scientists buy in to reincarnation.

Take Carl Sagan. The skeptic Sagan once asked the Dalai Lama what he would do if reincarnation, a fundamental tenet of his religion, were definitively disproved by science. The Dalai Lama answered, "If science can disprove reincarnation, Tibetan Buddhism would abandon reincarnation... but it's going to be mighty hard to disprove reincarnation."[12]

Despite those who have challenged its existence, today at least two-thirds of the world's citizens believe in reincarnation.

Indeed, if you are receptive to the concept of reincarnation, you are in good company. Some of the world's greatest thinkers have espoused the philosophy: philosophers Plato and Aristotle; statesmen Cicero and Julius Caesar; poets William Butler Yeats and Robert Frost; and scientists Ben Franklin and Thomas Edison.[13]

So, what can the belief in reincarnation offer us?

America's psychic diagnostician of the 1940s, Edgar Cayce, believed that we were affected by our past lives in many ways, not the least of which is through our individual abilities. Cayce said, "We don't have to remember past lives because we are the sum total of all our memories." He placed talent and interest firmly in the heredity of the soul rather than the heredity of one's grandparents.[14]

In the final analysis, whether or not we believe in the possibility of reincarnation, we would do well to follow the advice of our esteemed scientist, Albert Einstein. Einstein urged us "not to stop questioning. Curiosity has its own reason for existing. One cannot help but be in awe, when he contemplates the mysteries of eternity, of life, of the marvelous structure of reality."[15]

I believe in questioning the marvelous structure of reality, and I believe in reincarnation. As a regression therapist, I have helped countless individuals explore past lives, and I am certain that doing so has helped them unlock their true potential.

I have confidence that Cayce was right to place talent and interest in the heredity of the soul, which has led me to explore the past lives of celebrities in this book. If anything, reading this book may help you to realize that we all carry with us innate talents and interests from our past lives. The successes of celebrities are surely linked to what they carry in their souls. If you explore what's in yours, you may unlock your potential and add your star to life's walk of fame.

Introduction

* * *

Unearthing Celebrity Past-Life Clues

M any people who are curious about their past lives have a session or sessions with a hypnotherapist who facilitates an experience in which they get in touch with their subconscious minds where all memories are stored. Through the use of a series of relaxation techniques and open-ended questions, people may access their past lives, gain insights into other aspects of themselves, go to the root cause of issues and blockages, and transform their current lives.

A past-life regression is an intricate process, and without going through this process, people still are able to examine aspects of their lives and ferret out clues to their past lives. When pieced together, they can often get startling insight into a past life, patterns from the past, and fresh insights into their current lives, relationships, careers, talents, likes and dislikes.

How did I come to count on such clues as insights into past lives?

While working with Civil War and Renaissance reenactors while writing two books on the subject, for over a decade, I not only hypnotically regressed people to their past lives, but also I verified much of the memories that unfolded from their subconscious. My research led me to battlefields, cemeteries, and archives, as well as interviews with historians who specialize in fields such as 12th century French swords and medieval dress.

I traipsed through dusty Civil War battlefields wearing a hoop skirt; oogled the men on horseback in chain mail at Renaissance festivals; and wore a medieval, velvet "sideless surcote" first to a Society for Creative Anachronism (SCA) Twelfth Night gala and later for two weeks at the 24th annual Pennsic War in Pennsylvania. While portraying a Viking wearing a linen cap and tunic, I helped make leavened bread over a campfire at a "Military Through the Ages" competition for historical accuracy at Jamestown, Virginia, with a group of Living Historians.

In addition to the regressions I facilitated with my clients, those experiences gave me deep insight into the historical reenactors who were so passionate about their hobby and its time period that it bled into every area of their lives. Their passion affected how they played as children as well as their choice of professions and their pastimes. Their fascination with a certain time period influenced whether or not they joined the military, their personal relationships, and even the ways in which they planned their weddings or other celebrations. Their past lives became obvious to me even by their choice of clothing, where they lived, and how they decorated their homes. Civil War reenactors, for example, were mesmerized with the movie *Gettysburg*, while medieval reenactors loved *Braveheart*.

For over a decade, I observed these very obvious clues in my clients, and I then began to apply the same principles to my own life, as well as the lives of my friends, and even strangers I met on the street. This detective system eventually resulted in the book, *16 Clues to Your Past Lives.* Because "the woman on the street" like me, does not have much interaction with A-list actors and actresses, and because I was curious to know celebrities on a more multidimensional level, I decided to apply the suggestions from my book *16 Clues to Your Past Lives* to celebrities' lives and see what I could learn.

As I sifted through personal information about the celebrities that was readily available in the public domain, some clues to their past lives immediately jumped out at me. Other clues were subtle but gained significance once applied in context with additional clues. For example, the fact that Tom Hanks collects typewriters seems to correlate with his interest in war and the military. Piecing several clues together, one might postulate that he could have been a war correspondent.

In the case of actors, I particularly looked at the roles in which they were consistently cast, had chosen, or for which they were critically acclaimed or had made an impact.

A major clue that was consistent with many performers was their interest in acting as a youngster, as well as how they spent their time during their youth. Another was how many of these performers seemed to express talents beyond their experience. If there are no "artistic genes" in the family tree, then one could easily question the theory of genetic memory, or the fact that talent was likely passed down through the genes.

Shirley Temple is one such example. At the age of three, with no family members in show business, she was chosen for a screen test and could sing, dance, and act alongside the "greats" of her day. She had the natural ability to mimic dance steps and exuded an amazing star quality as a child.[16]

American psychic diagnostician Edgar Cayce placed talents firmly in the heredity of the soul. He attributed child genius and great talent to skill development through many lifetimes of practice.[17] If, indeed, this is true, we are blessed to be the audience-recipients of lifetimes of dedication by an actress such as Meryl Streep. If she makes it look so easy, maybe it's because she has so embraced her talents over lifetimes that performing is truly natural for her.

While reviewing the roles of the actors and actresses I've examined in this book, I took particular interest in what historical time periods they consistently acted, as well as any patterns that repeated, either in their roles—e.g. if they were cast as a cowboy, underdog, or bully—or patterns in their personal lives. This could also include irrational fears, such as fear of heights.

Sometimes it could be significant where a celebrity holds her wedding festivities or where s/he chooses to live, whether on a ranch or island. It is even significant how celebrities choose to decorate their homes or what clothes they feel comfortable wearing.

Major relationships, such as spouses, best friends, and co-workers would most likely be significant since past-life wisdom posits that people return time after time with a close circle of individuals that includes family, mates and co-workers. Too, strong feelings of "love at first sight" can be a trigger for the remembrance of having known another before and thus immediately accessing a sense of familiarity, comfort, and, often, romantic passion.

I also looked at the celebrities' "synchronistic" experiences, i.e. meaningful coincidences. Lana Turner, for example, was at a soda shop in Hollywood when the right person "discovered" her. And, while still in film school, Matthew McConaughey met a casting director in a Texas bar and was cast in a movie.

Significant past-life clues can be found in a celebrity's personal life, education, interests, and hobbies and even humanitarian work. Angelina Jolie's global work is noteworthy when looking at her possible past lives. Both Meryl Streep and Matthew McConaughey seriously considered becoming lawyers...perhaps another past-life clue.

Journey with me as we take a novel look at celebrities who grace the silver screen and the covers of magazines, those who entertain us, inform us, and inspire us. Observe how each clue from their present days can form a meaningful framework through which to view some of the possible past-lives that touched the souls of these talented, skilled, committed achievers.

As you make this journey and are able to identify the clues, take an assessment of your own past-life clues and those of the people around you. If you'd like further guidance on your own self-exploration and thought stimulation to trigger your own memories and how to piece them together, check out *16 Clues to Your Past Lives*! Happy journeys!

Chapter 1

* * *

Meryl Streep

If she hadn't overslept and missed her interview for acceptance into law school, the world would have never known what an artistic loss it would have been not to know Meryl Streep as an actress. Deciding the missed interview was destiny, Streep, widely acclaimed as perhaps the greatest living actress, refocused her attention on her acting career. Besides holding the record for the most Oscar nominations at nineteen, of which she has won three, Streep also holds the record for the most Golden Globe nominations at 29 in all.

Streep was born in New Jersey to a mother who kept an art studio behind the house and a father, a drug company executive, who loved to play the piano while her mother sang. Family home videos show Streep hamming it up as a youngster. At twelve, after singing at a school recital, she took opera training for four years.

Streep found that she preferred acting. She discovered it at Bernards High School. She also had time to be a cheerleader and homecoming queen before moving on to study drama at Vassar. While at Vassar, her drama professor said, "I don't think anyone ever taught Meryl acting. She really taught herself."[1] After graduation, she moved on to Dartmouth and then Yale, where she appeared in more than thirty productions with the Yale Repertory Theater.

Her next career move was on to Broadway. TV and film followed. By her second film, *The Deer Hunter*, Streep had earned her first Oscar nomination.

That same year,1978, she won her first Emmy for her lead role in the TV miniseries *Holocaust*, bringing her to a new level of national recognition. Taking place in World War II era Germany, in *Holocaust* Streep portrayed a German woman compromised by the political order and her commitment to her marriage to a Jewish husband. During the filming, Streep, who is part German and Swiss, travelled to Germany and Austria, leaving behind her romantic interest, John Cazale, who was dying.

Later, Streep would be so determined to get the Holocaust role of Sophie in *Sophie's Choice* that she is said to have obtained a pirated copy of the script. After reading it, she implored the director to hire her by dramatically falling to her knees.[2] He did. Streep, who mastered a Polish accent, did such a heart-wrenching portrayal of a young mother in a Nazi concentration camp that she earned her first Academy Award for Best Actress. Streep found the scene where she has to choose between her son and daughter so emotional that she refused to redo it.

Another Academy Award role was portraying British Prime Minister Margaret Thatcher in *Iron Lady*. Known for being a perfectionist when preparing for roles, Streep took diction lessons to alter her tone, articulation and delivery to be able to reproduce Thatcher's vocal style. Streep became known for her ability to master almost any accent. She also observed British MPs at work at the House of Commons.

The role of the female Prime Minister was appealing to Streep because of issues surrounding women and power, both the gaining and losing of power. Although she didn't agree with all her politics, Streep admired Thatcher for being willing to find solutions and take a stand, even if it wasn't popular. With all the images people had about Thatcher, Streep wanted to tap into Thatcher, the human being, and to feel what it must have been like to have been her.[3] After Thatcher died, Streep formally criticized Thatcher's tough handling of financial measures.

Streep, who is an advocate of women's rights, reproductive rights, and female empowerment, donated her salary from *The Iron Lady* to the National Women's History Museum.

More than two decades before, after reviewing the script for *Kramer vs. Kramer*, she disputed the portrayal of her female character who was judged to be immoral because of her divorce and ensuing fight to retain her children. Streep was allowed to write some of her own dialogue and negotiated a script rewrite.

In her personal life, Streep can't imagine a life without being married and having children. "I think I was wired for family...I can't imagine living single," she says[4] She's been married to sculptor Don Gummer since 1978 and the couple has four children. "I'd be dead, emotionally at least, if I hadn't met my husband."[5] As for work and family, Streep says she has a "holistic need to work and have huge ties of love in my life. I can't imagine eschewing one for the other."[6]

Streep believes the key to success in work and relationships is listening. "Listening is everything. It's the whole deal... It's where you learn everything."[7]

So, what kinds of roles has the most prominent actress of our time played in past lives? First and foremost, Streep

has been an actress many times. The actress, who is known
to have a photographic memory and can remember her lines
with one reading, has clearly been a performer many times
before. Psychic diagnostician Edgar Cayce believed that it
took about 33 lifetimes to develop talent to the level of a
Bach or Beethoven. If this is the case, then many lives of
dedication could be a reason why Streep appears to be such
a natural.

For the big screen, Streep has spoken with accents that
include Danish, English, Australian, and Italian as well as
Irish-American, Minnesotan and Bronx.   Although she
chalks it up to just listening, she has a natural aptitude for accents.[8] As far as past-life explanations, she could have lived
in, or travelled to, a variety of countries. She also could have
lived on a trade route or cosmopolitan city where she heard
and paid attention to a variety of dialects.

Streep has been compared to a chameleon who can lose
herself in her role, and transform herself, even physically,
into a Margaret Thatcher or a Julia Child. Whether playing the Prime Minister, a whistleblower, a Danish plantation
owner in Kenya, a music teacher in Harlem, or a nun in the
Bronx, Streep compassionately identifies with and portrays
her characters' humanity.

Over lifetimes, Streep has developed a deep grasp of human nature, by paying attention to the psychology of being.
Is this a reason why Streep can be a clear vessel for the roles
she plays? Whatever the case may be, Streep has had a variety of lifetimes and clearly has the wisdom to hold fast to the
importance of the individual no matter what role she is in.

Two of her most impacting roles, both in a miniseries
and on the big screen, were related to the Holocaust in Nazi
Germany. The fact that Streep fought for the role as a mother in a concentration camp in *Sophie's Choice* is significant.
Streep even attacked Walt Disney as being "anti-Semitic." It's

entirely possible that Streep could have been in a concentra-tion camp in World War II.

Given the fact that she is so devoted to motherhood, it's also possible that she lost a child during that life or in anoth-er one. Perhaps that's why she refused to redo the "choice" scene, saying it took so much out of her emotionally. Was she tapping into haunting past-life memories?

It is also possible that being a performer in other life-times, Streep had to forgo a family, and this time she has been determined to perform and have a family too.

As for playing the role of Thatcher, perhaps that trig-gered a political nerve. Streep clearly voiced her own opin-ions that were in conflict with the Prime Minister's politics. She was initially focused on going to law school. If she wasn't a decision-maker for the masses, she may have influenced a powerful person or people in other lives. Maybe she fought for the underdog. Perhaps she was a woman who balked at the defenseless of women, their status, and their inability to have a voice.

This time she has no trouble speaking out to defend women and their rights.

Finally, Streep loves music and singing. She often gets into character listening to classical music. She studied to be an opera singer at the age of twelve. For her role as a music teacher in *Music of the Heart*, she learned to play the violin in eight weeks by practicing six hours a day. After her Grammy nomination for her song from the soundtrack of *Mamma Mia*, Streep said she wanted to be a musician, if she wasn't an actress. Streep is scheduled to play opera singer Maria Callas in an upcoming HBO film. It's easy to envision Streep as an opera singer and classical musician in several other lifetimes.

The world is fortunate to have witnessed the genius that Streep has exhibited on screen and stage in this lifetime and other past lives. Streep has not only brought forward her soul's acting and musical abilities but her compassionate observance of humanity and her advocacy for their needs.

Chapter 2

* * *

Nicole Kidman

It's no surprise that Nicole Kidman gravitated to the movie *Railway Man* given its theme of forgiveness. In the film, Kidman plays a dowdy nurse who fights to help her husband, a psychologically damaged British World War II prisoner of war, rehabilitate himself after returning home. Her husband, played by Colin Firth, must begin his healing journey by forgiving his Japanese torturer and Kidman's character stands by him as he struggles to forgive.

In real life, the award-winning actress's mother was a nursing instructor and her father a clinical psychologist and biochemist. Kidman's parents were anti-Vietnam protestors, and she participated in her parents' campaigns by passing out pamphlets on street corners. It's no wonder then, that Kidman would like the theme of reconciliation in *Railway*

Man. By the time she was 19, Kidman starred in the TV miniseries *Vietnam.*

As a teen, Kidman temporarily halted her education to help provide for the family and took up massage therapy while her mother was going through breast cancer. Perhaps the screen role of nurse or caretaker comes easily to her. Could this have been a past life?

Perhaps with her father's influence, she has had an understanding or innate feeling for psychology, depression, and the psychology of war. Kidman attributes her sense of empathy to her father. She says she errs on the side of understanding and gentleness."[1] Her acting coach Susan Bateman describes Kidman as "being a deeply compassionate person, which is central to her talent."[2]

In Kidman's academy award-winning portrayal of Virginia Woolf, she plunged into episodes of mental illness and battled with depression. She says that "she's not interested in playing it safe, but goes where she needs to go—emotionally, tonally or psychologically."[3]

In the movie *Cold Mountain,* Kidman played a Southern woman who was separated from her love during the Civil War and had to eke out an existence. It is very likely that she has had a lifetime or lifetimes as a woman who has had to deal with loss and psychological damage associated with the return of her soldier from war. Given her life clues, it's possible that her past lives include the American Civil War and/or World War II.

In addition to past lives related to caretaking and war, past-life believers may identify Kidman as having been an actress in one or more lives. Kidman says she is lucky because she knew from a very young age, as a schoolgirl, that she wanted to be an actress.

The Kidman family moved to Sydney when she was three, and Kidman soon discovered that she loved ballet, mime and drama. At five, Kidman's first acting role was as a sheep in a school nativity play, and by ten, she had joined an acting school. Her dedication to acting led to Australian Film Industry Award nominations when she was just fourteen. Kidman appeared on Sesame Street, and she won an American Film Institute Best Actress award at age seventeen for the TV mini-series *Vietnam*. Such accolades at an early age are most definitely a past-life indicator.

These days, Kidman is a humanitarian and peace activist; in 2013, as a UN Goodwill Ambassador, she received an award from the Cinema for Peace Foundation in Berlin, Germany. Kidman believes that when the world is in so much turmoil, people need the arts to uplift them.

Award-winning actress, activist, and Goodwill Ambassador Kidman is above all things a devoted wife and mother. She is never happier than when she's spending time with her family. She is married to country music star Keith Urban and the couple has two daughters. From her first marriage to Tom Cruise, Kidman has two teenage children.

Kidman has most likely been with Urban and her children in a past life. Her past-life return to a very public marriage with Cruise also is extremely likely. She and ex-husband Cruise made three movies together, one or which was the Irish epic *Far and Away*. Perhaps they shared a past life in Ireland.

As for actor Colin Firth, he refers to Kidman as his "work wife" now that they are about to shoot their fourth movie together. He appreciates their connection, her versatility, and the choices she makes. Firth's comment begs the question for all celebrities: "Have the actors and actresses who work together had past lives together?" Past-life believers might argue that Kidman's repeated work with Firth is no accident. They are likely drawn to one another from more than this lifetime.

We should also pay attention to what we joke about, another past-life clue. It appears that in one lifetime Kidman was a caretaker of a veteran returned from war. And while Kidman's childhood acting dreams are very real from this life, it's possible her passion stems from past lives as well. Such passion and talent has allowed Kidman to realize and wildly exceed her dreams.

Chapter 3

* * *

Colin Firth

The theme in *Railway Man*, a true story of torture and the resulting post-traumatic stress from being a prisoner of war, is a past-life trigger not only for those who have endured this type of suffering in various wars, but also for the families who love them. Upon viewing the atrocious, brutal treatment, such as that received by World War II British soldier Eric Lomax, who was forced by the Japanese to work on the notorious "Death Railway" in the jungles of Thailand, those who resonate on the deepest levels may be reminded of the cruelties of war that they may have experienced, in World War II or in another timeframe.

Actors, too, may be emotionally impacted by their involvement in such a movie. In fact, perhaps one reason they are drawn to a particular script and its scenario or historic time period is because they have been there before. It's entirely

possible that is one reason why top stars choose to be involved in a certain movie. Firth can have his pick of movies,
but he connected to something in the story of *Railway Man*.
Could it have been the traumatization of war that piqued
Firth's interest?

A theme in Firth's early works was playing those trauma-
tized by war. Firth portrayed real-life British soldier Robert
Lawrence in the 1988 BBC drama *Tumbledown*, which portrays Lawrence's struggles with his disabilities after returning
from the Falkland's War. Six years later, Firth had a supporting role in *The English Patient* as Geoffrey Clifton, an operative for British Intelligence. And, more recently playing the
older, dysfunctional Lomax, Firth was particularly interested
in the torment and harm that war inflicts on relationships.

Another theme of the movie *Railway Man* is reconciliation. It is a real testament that for acts as cruel as the torture
of prisoners of war and their continuing life of psychological
torture, a person, such as the real-life Lomax, would be able
to forgive his Japanese torturer. After an embattled internal
struggle, Lomax forgives his captor. His captor says, "Maybe
we both lived for this day."[1] It is clear to them, as well as it is
to the audience, that the ravages of war have devastated both
men.

It seems that Firth is particularly good at appearing as
an emotionally withdrawn character. Could this be a theme
in one, or more, of Firth's past lives? Did Firth return home
after a war such as World War II, only to fight another battle
of psychological survival? Is this why he is so believable in a
role such as the one he performed in *Railway Man*? Is this
why he is cast in such roles?

It's important as well when examining past-life clues to
take a look at one's accolades. In 2011, Firth won numerous awards, including an Oscar, for playing the historical
figure King George VI in *The King's Speech*, which accounts
King George's struggles to overcome a speech impediment.

Interestingly, Firth's father taught history in England. Perhaps history is in Firth's genes, but it is likely Firth was a prominent historical figure in a past life as well; for, given the way he fell deeply into the role of King George VI one must wonder if it was his soul remembering.

In addition to examining the roles Firth plays in order to gain past-life clues, another past-life clue is to examine what he did at an early age. Firth's first acting experience came in infant's school when he played Jack Frost at a Christmas pantomime. He spent two years at the Drama Center in Chalk Farm where he was discovered while playing *Hamlet*. And by the time he was fourteen, Firth had already decided he wanted to be a professional actor, having attended drama workshops from the age of ten. The fact that Firth was acting from the age of five could indicate knowledge, interest, and talent from a past life. In other words, such information could indicate that Firth has been an actor in a past life.

Movies and messages such as these can help to heal actors as well as those who view their films, and with such experiences the collective consciousness heals as love replaces hatred and forgiveness replaces vengeance. In other words, with the help of the arts and the performers who grace our stages and screens, we can all access parts of our souls that are longing to be healed. The soul carries memory with it from one lifetime to another, and the memory may contain pain and sorrow. One of the major karmic lessons to be learned sooner or later is how to reach into past lives to heal the current one. Actors do this for themselves through the roles to which they commit, and they do it for the audience through the emotion their performances draw out of us.

Chapter 4

* * *

Robert De Niro

Academy-award winning actor Robert De Niro, has an innate ability to assume the character in his movies. He was raised in the Little Italy section of New York's Greenwich Village by two artist parents whose parents immigrated from Italy and Ireland. His parents divorced when he was a youngster.

As a child, De Niro loved reading plays, and at ten years old he fell in love with acting when he played the cowardly lion in a local production of *The Wizard of Oz*. In ninth grade, he attended New York's High School of Music and Art, and later after being inspired by the movies, he told a friend he was going to be a film actor. Everyone was shocked when he dropped out of high school to join a gang. His nickname was "Bobby Milk" because he was as pale as milk. He then joined Stella Adler's Conservatory and Lee Strasberg's Actors Studio.

De Niro got his break when he ran into Martin Scorsese at a party in their Little Italy neighborhood. They realized they had seen each other before on numerous occasions, and the two hit it off. Scorsese cast him as a small-time criminal in 1973's *Mean Streets*. Was this meeting just the beginning of a long, fruitful working relationship, or could it have been a fateful soul connection from a past-life?

Mean Streets caught Francis Ford Coppola's attention, and De Niro was thus cast in *The Godfather Part II*. In preparation for his role, De Niro spent four months in Sicily learning multiple dialects. He stood on street corners and tape-recorded gangs' conversations.

De Niro was so believable as Vito Corleone in *The Godfather Part II* that he was awarded an Oscar for Best Supporting Actor. Although he is only one-quarter Italian, De Niro feels a deep connection with his Italian roots. He has even been inducted into the Italian-American Hall of Fame. Could De Niro have a Sicilian mafia past-life connection? It seems likely.

Marlon Brando was one of De Niro's boyhood idols, and he emulated Brando's dark, character-driven style in many of his films—De Niro immersed himself in his characters with a brutal intensity. Interestingly, both of De Niro's Oscar-winning performances involved Brando: in *The Godfather Part II*, De Niro played the younger version of Brando's character; and in *Raging Bull*, he recited Brando's famous lines from *On the Waterfront*, which were performed nearly thirty years before. De Niro and Brando were onscreen together only once in *The Score*, but they're connection is clear. Did Brando serve as De Niro's mentor in a former life? Perhaps.

There's also his convincing portrayal of American gangsters. In addition to his role as Corleone, De Niro played a cruel mobster in *Goodfellas*, a boy divided between his father and the local mob in *A Bronx Tale*, a drug dealer in the theatre production *Cuba and His Teddy Bear*, and the bat-wielding Al Capone in *The Untouchables*. Even in more recent humorous roles, such as *Analyze This*, De Niro is a mafia don.

About these mobster characters, De Niro says, "The characters that I play are real so they have as much right to be portrayed as any other characters."[1]

Until recently, De Niro has been typecast as a brutally violent, angry, depressed man. Coupled with the intensity with which he performs using his method acting, the audience benefits from portrayals that seem as real as reality can be. For example, De Niro gained sixty pounds and learned how to box so well for his role in *Raging Bull* that he could have boxed professionally. In one sparring scene, he accidentally broke Joe Pesci's rib. He says, "I just can't fake acting. I want to deal with all the facts of the character, thin or fat."[2]

For his role in *Taxi Driver*, De Niro took various shifts driving taxis for several weeks, and while preparing for his role in *Cape Fear*, he paid a dentist $5,000 to make his teeth look awful. After the shoot, he paid $20,000 to have them corrected. For *The Deer Hunter*, he played pool and drank with mill workers in order to take on the character, Sergeant Mike Vronsky.

De Niro seems to have an inherent aptitude to portray his characters, and he also is so driven that he has even asked to rehearse on Sundays.

De Niro believes that there's no place like New York. "It's the most exciting city in the world. I like New York because I can still walk the streets and sit down in a restaurant and observe people."[3] Given his love of the city, it's no surprise that De Niro has built up the area around Greenwich, particularly since 9-11. His film studio TriBeCa Productions is based there, he started the Tribeca Film Festival there, and he co-owns a hotel along with several restaurants in the area.

De Niro also values roots: his Italian roots, his New York City roots, and his family roots. De Niro has honored the abstract expressionist art of his late father in an HBO documentary. De Niro's father is said to have wanted to be an artist since kindergarten; he loved France and the French artists, was obsessed with Greta Garbo, and lived and painted in France. De Niro's dad was most likely a French painter in another lifetime, and Robert De Niro Sr. clearly passed down his artistic genes to his son, who transformed them into his own kind of art.

If there are past lives, then based on the patterns I've discussed in this chapter, it's clear that De Niro was an actor in several of them. He likely lived in Italy and in New York in his past lives, and it's probable that he ran with some very tough crowds in former incarnations.

Chapter 5

* * *

Billy Crystal

Billy Crystal has spent much of his life making people laugh. A born entertainer and the youngest of three boys, Crystal liked to sing, dance, and act with his brothers for the family in their living room. "I was the little Jerry Lewis," he said.[33]

In addition to his love of comedy, by the age of five, Crystal dreamed of being a professional baseball player. At the age of eight, Crystal saw his first Yankees game with his father. The two shared this passion for the sport, which his father had played during college. They spent Sundays playing baseball and watching games together.

While supporting Crystal's love of baseball, to pique his son's interest in comedy at an early age, Crystal's dad, Jack—a jazz concert producer, co-founder of the Commodore record label, and owner of a famous record store on New York City's

42nd Street—brought home recordings of comics like Laurel and Hardy and Sid Caesar that Crystal and his two brothers studied. Crystal was also influenced by TV shows like *The Honeymooners.*[34]

In high school, Crystal says he was the class comedian—the one who talked the class clown into dropping his pants. By sixteen, he began touring clubs and honing his humor based on his own experiences and those of his audiences.

After high school, Crystal earned a baseball scholarship. He then changed schools to be near his future wife, a dancer, who he described as "his first and only date." At New York University, he studied to be a film director under Martin Scorsese.

It was then that Crystal returned to his love of comedy. Crystal claims that instead of baseball, he chose comedy because "God made [him] short."

As a struggling comedian, he was a substitute teacher, and, as "Mr. Mom," Crystal took his first daughter to rehearsals with him. He became the opening act for musicians such as Barry Manilow.

He then moved to Hollywood where he acted in the TV sitcom *Soap,* which led to gigs on *Saturday Night Live.* Crystal's fame grew, and he starred in several movies, such as *When Harry Met Sally, City Slickers,* and *Analyze This.* He also has hosted the Academy Awards nine times.

Despite his success as a comedian and actor, Crystal never strayed from his love of baseball. In the movie *City Slickers,* Crystal wears a New York Mets baseball cap. In *Running Scared,* he wears a Cubs' jersey; and in *Parental Guidance,* he's the announcer for a Minor League Baseball team.

Earlier, in one of his first television appearances, Crystal met his idol, Yankee outfielder Mickey Mantle, in person and asked Mantle to re-sign the same program Mantle had signed for Crystal once after a game. Crystal became good friends with him and later wrote Mantle's eulogy.

Crystal directed and produced the HBO film *61** based on the relationship between Mantle and Roger Maris and their attempts to break Babe Ruth's home run record. The movie received twelve Emmy nominations. Crystal succeeded again, this time marrying his love of film with his love of baseball. What's more, he felt that working on the film connected him to his father.

Although a lifelong Yankee fan, Crystal is part owner of the Arizona Diamondbacks baseball team, which earned him a World Series ring in 2001 for their defeat against the Yankees. In 2008, Crystal signed a 24-hour minor league contract with the New York Yankees and was invited to work out with the team at spring training. In honor of his 60th birthday, Crystal wore uniform number 60 and led off as designated hitter, managing to contact the ball.

With Crystal's passions and talents in comedy, acting and baseball, it seems likely that he has been connected with both of these in past lives.

Chapter 6

* * *

Jon Favreau

For comedian, writer, actor, and director Jon Favreau, food is clearly important. After all, he wrote, directed and acted in *Chef*, a movie about a gourmet chef who starts a Cuban food truck after being fired from an upscale restaurant.

For the movie, Favreau trained at a culinary school and cooked at home with his three kids. He says he felt lucky to be trained by the great chefs Wolfgang Puck and David Chang, whom he reverently refers to as "rock stars."[1] As a result of the film, Favreau claims that cooking is now so much a hobby that he has remodeled his kitchen into a commercial kitchen complete with a flat top grill and a pizza oven.

Favreau not only enjoys cooking, but also he sees it as a way of bringing people together.[2]

Was Favreau influenced by the movie *Chef*, or was *Chef* a trigger to recall a past life as a chef? Of course, he wrote the movie before being coached by the chefs. As a writer-actor, it could be the case that he was already a chef in his creative mind, long before he wrote and performed the role.

Past-life believers may not find it surprising that food has been a theme running through Favreau's personal and professional lives.

Favreau grew up in Queens, New York, the son of two teachers. In high school, he became interested in acting and, weighing 280 pounds, imagined he could be the next John Belushi or John Candy. His first career move was to Chicago where he found himself washing dishes at the Second City restaurant. Eventually, Favreau moved to Los Angeles and lost 80 pounds.

After his father gave him screenwriting software, Favreau wrote a semi-autobiographical script, *Swingers,* about being a comedian in Hollywood and trying to pick up stunning women at late-night diners. Favreau, along with his real-life close friend, actor Vince Vaughn, starred in it, and the film became an indie favorite.

Another creation of Favreau's that involves food was the cable television series *Dinner for Five.* As creator and producer, he wanted to show movie people, who are smart and interesting, sitting around a dinner table as real people talking about real topics. The show aired on IFC for four years.

In sum, there's no doubt food has been an important part of Favreau's life. Aside from his early goal to be a funny fat guy, a connection to food has been interwoven into his career since the first movie he wrote and acted in as well as a television series he created and produced. Then, he upped the ante and wrote a movie about a gourmet chef and was trained to act just like one. Favreau now is taking cooking personally—right into his kitchen where his three kids, wife, and company can look forward to the culinary feasts he will be dishing out.

Very possibly, Favreau has rediscovered his love for cooking from a former lifetime.

Chapter 7

***

Russell Crowe

If there are past lives, it's no secret Russell Crowe was an actor before. But to delve into his other lives, let's look at the historic epic roles in which he is cast consistently and the impact they have made.

Crowe achieved international attention for his role as the Roman general, Maximus, in Ridley Scott's 2000 historic epic film *Gladiator* for which he won the Academy Award for Best Actor and earned twelve other award nominations.

When he was asked what attracts him to prospective films, Crowe says he responds to a call that says, "It's 185 A.D. You're a Roman general. That's something my imagination can get a hold of."[1] Maybe he resonates to such roles because he has held similar, real-life roles before. In fact, Crow wanted his performance in *Gladiator* to be so credible, that he rebuffed studio demands for a sex scene. "I'm sorry boys, but it doesn't suit the character. We can't be avenging the death of the wife and child, and stop for sex along the way."[2]

From his performance in *Gladiator* alone, past-life believers can easily agree that Crowe held a position in the Roman army in a past life. Aside from his film portrayal of a Roman general, another clue affirms this: as a teen, Crowe formed a band. Can you guess its name? Roman Antix.

Crowe was born in New Zealand and, as a youngster his family moved to Australia. Because his parents were caterers for movie shoots, he hung around film sets and developed a passion for acting. By six, he had acted in the TV series *Spyforce*. He then took a twelve-year break and tried a music career as a rockabilly singer.

At 21, Crowe was working in theatre in Australia. While considering studying at the National Institute of Dramatic Art, he talked to the head of technical support there. He told Crowe doing so would be a waste of time. He said, "You already do the things you go there to learn, and you've been doing it for most of your life."[3] Crowe followed the advice, and after his young success in Australia, Crowe starred in a Canadian production before moving on to concentrate on American films.

It was the Roman epic *Gladiator* that propelled Crowe into the public's consciousness.

Interestingly, Crowe was invited to perform in another historical epic: Oliver Stone's 2004 *Alexander*. In it, Crowe would have portrayed the 4th century B.C. Macedonian conqueror, Alexander the Great. Although Crowe turned down the lead role, it is said that he was director Stone's dream choice. Could that be because it's easy for audiences to believe that Crowe draws out from within him the memory of these ancient warriors?

Crowe was also the first choice for the role of Stonewall Jackson in Ron Maxwell's 2003 Civil War epic, *Gods and Generals,* but Crowe later dropped out. Jackson, one of the most well known Confederate generals, is still revered by many Americans. Did Maxwell, like Stone and Scott, sense something about Crowe's military leadership abilities and thus rely upon the fact that Crowe would be believable in these leadership roles?

Crowe is connected to a number of films set during war, and about war he has stated the following, "In wars, no one wins, everyone loses. There are no heroes, there's only dead people. Movies can really change things. It becomes an educational process and I think that's the healthiest way of attacking anything."[3] Crowe's perspective on war sounds like it comes from real life experience.

Instead of starring in *Gods and Generals* in 2003, Crowe portrayed British naval officer Jack Aubrey in another epic historical drama, *Master and Commander: The Far Side of the World*. The film takes place in 1805, during the Napoleonic Wars and was nominated for ten Oscars. In *Master and Commander*, we again see Crowe accessing his internal warrior, and, interestingly, he also accessed his musical talents: Crowe took violin lessons to play violin in the movie. As well, in the movie adaptation of the popular musical, *Les Miserables*, which takes place at the peak of the French Revolution, Crowe portrayed French Inspector Javert and employs his singing talents.

In addition to his affinity for music, since his youth, Crowe has had a special love of horses. "There are some horses that you have a deeper connection with," he says.[4] Crowe sometimes finds it difficult to leave his horse when a film involving horses ends. Past-life believers can easily see a connection to the warrior soul in Crowe: until recently, many soldiers and warriors rode horses.

Crowe was sought after by directors for roles such as the Roman general in *Gladiator*, the Macedonian leader Alexander the Great, American Civil War Confederate General Jackson, Napoleonic War British naval officer

Aubrey and Inspector Javert in the French Revolution. If all the directors of these historic films would choose Crowe as an epic military leader, then it is entirely possible that he was indeed a powerful military leader in one or more of his past lives.

Chapter 8

* * *

Robert Duvall

A ctor and director Robert Duvall has the distinction of being named the most versatile actor in the world by the Guinness Book of World Records.

He was born in San Diego, California, in 1931, and at the age of ten, his family moved to Annapolis, Maryland. Duvall's father moved up the ranks of the U.S. Navy and became a Rear Admiral. Self-described as a "navy brat," Duvall spent several summers on an uncle's ranch in Montana where he developed a love for horses. His Montana ranch experiences must have made an impact on him; he was later to win his only Oscar for his role in *Tender Mercies* as country singer Mac Sledge. Duvall has also won four Golden Globes including one for his role in *Tender Mercies* and another for his work on the television miniseries *Lonesome Dove*.

As country western singer Sledge in *Tender Mercies* in 1983, Duvall was said to have written some of the music and insisted he do his own singing. Duvall said, "What's the point if you're not going to do your own singing?"[1] His co-star, Tess Harper, said that she never got to know Duvall because he stayed in character.[2] Director Bruce Beresford felt his skin crawl when he saw Duvall transformed into his character. "Duvall totally and utterly becomes that person to a degree which is uncanny," he said.[3]

Six years after *Tender Mercies* was released, Duvall appeared in the TV miniseries *Lonesome Dove* as Gus McCrae, a Texas Ranger. For the role, Duvall was trained to use Walker revolvers by Texas marksman Joe Bowman. Duvall said, "I nailed a very specific, individual guy who represents something important in our history of the western movement. After that, I felt I could retire, that'd I'd done something."[4]

Duvall did everything but retire after his role in *Lonesome Dove*. He went on to be featured in both film and television productions, including his most recent role in *The Judge*.

In 2011, he appeared at a charity event themed "An Evening with a Texas Legend" in Houston, Texas. Duvall does not hail from Texas, but given his memorable role as McCrae, he has become legendary in the state. Of all his many and varied roles, Duvall said that the particular role of McCrae was his favorite. Perhaps Duvall has been a cowboy or western singer in another life.

In addition to Duvall's connection to the country-western identity, Duvall's life reflects an association with the Civil War. He owns a large estate in rural Virginia, which he describes as "the last station before heaven."[5] A number of Civil War skirmishes were fought on his property, and shells and other artifacts have been found there. In fact, several scenes in the epic Civil War drama *Gods and Generals* were filmed on his property. In the movie, Duvall played his own ancestor, Confederate General Robert E Lee. Duvall also received an Honorary Doctorate of Arts from Shenandoah Conservatory in Winchester, Virginia, a university linked with the Civil War.

There very likely could be a Civil War officer theme for Robert Duvall, who not only lives on Civil War land but also played his ancestor Robert E Lee in a Civil War epic drama. Duvall has also fought for Civil War battlefield preservation.

In 2009, Duvall spoke for historic preservation against WalMart's proposal to build a store across the road from the entrance to the Civil War Wilderness Battlefield National Park in Virginia.

But Duvall's past-life patterns don't stop at the Civil War or the Wild West. He also has a fascination with all things Argentina, so much so that it clearly transcends the fact that his fourth wife is Argentinean. In 2005, after seven years together, he married Luciana Pedraza, 41 years his junior, who, by chance, he met in a bakery in Argentina.

Duvall loves Argentina, can speak Spanish fluently, travels there at least five times a year, and owns a home there.

"There's a place called La Biela, it's my favorite corner in the world." Duvall loves to sit at a coffee shop near the Recoleta and people-watch, whether it's at 3 a.m. or 8 a.m. "Going to Argentina, going to Buenos Aires, I like it more there than any place else," he says.[7]

Since 2001, Pedraza and Duvall have assisted families in Northern Argentina through renovations of homes, schools, and medical facilities. Duvall and Pedraza have also been helping Latin America's poorest women.

Duvall has a passion for all things Argentinian, including tango dancing. He is a prolific dancer and owns Tango Studio, which has locations in both Argentina and in the U.S. He also produced, directed, and acted with his wife in 2003's *Assassination Tango*, with the majority of the filming done in Buenos Aires.

Past-life believers might suggest that because Duvall is an excellent character actor, he, was probably an actor in a former life. Duvall also was most likely a western cowboy, a Confederate Civil War officer from Virginia, and an Argentinean in past lives. It's possible that he knew his wife Pedraza in the past, danced the tango and drank espresso around the neighborhood, Recoleta. Given clues in this lifetime, it's even safe to guess that Duvall was an Argentinian gaucho, a South American cowboy in a past life.

Chapter 9

* * *

Donald Sterling

Former owner of the Los Angeles Clippers, Donald Sterling's history of discrimination has been splashed across the pages of the media for nearly a year. Sterling's racist mind-set became public when his then- girlfriend released a tape she had recorded of one of their conversations. 80-year-old lawyer and billionaire real estate investor, Sterling was banned by the NBA after the release of the tape in April 2014 on account of its racist commentary.

His now ex-girlfriend, V. Stiviano, taped a conversation about his reaction to her posting a photo of herself with basketball great Magic Johnson on Instagram. In the audio recording, Sterling allegedly tells Stiviano, "It bothers me a lot that you want to broadcast that you're associating with black people."[1] I don't think I need to point out that the NBA is a league that predominantly employs African American athletes, so clearly it was problematic for Sterling to make such a comment, especially given his role as owner of an NBA team.

Nearly fifty years his junior, Stiviano recently legally changed her name from María Vanessa Perez because she said she had not been "fully accepted because of my race." On the tape, a voice that sounds distinctly like Sterling says, "You're supposed to be a delicate white or a delicate Latina girl." Responding to him, she says, "You're in love with me. And I'm black and Mexican whether you like it or not."[2] Given his racial attitudes, some might question Sterling's relationship with V.

Could Sterling's history of discrimination go back further than this lifetime?

Sterling was born Donald Tokowitz in Chicago to parents who were Ashkenazi Jewish immigrants. His family moved to Los Angeles when he was two. Sterling began practicing law when Jews were discriminated against in prominent law firms. His greatest financial success came in business enterprises in Los Angeles area real estate.

In 1981, Sterling bought the Clippers for $12.5 million. At thirty-three seasons of ownership, Sterling was the longest tenured owner in the NBA. After Sterling moved the Clippers from San Diego to Los Angeles, the team began to become a contender for the title, winning 47 games in the 2005-2006 season, for example.

Sterling's history of discrimination flared its ugly head when, in 2003, he paid a huge settlement to eighteen tenants who claimed discrimination and cited racial statements such as, "black people smell and attract vermin" and "Hispanics just smoke and hang around the building," as well as Sterling's alleged intent to rent only to Korean tenants because "they will pay the rent and live in whatever conditions I give them."[3] In 2006 and 2009, Sterling was again sued for housing discrimination for using race as a factor in his rental practices.

In February 2009, former longtime Clippers executive Elgin Baylor sued Sterling for employment discrimination on the basis of age and race. The lawsuit alleged that Sterling told Baylor that he wanted to fill his team with "poor black boys from the South and a white head coach." Baylor referred to Sterling's vision of the Clippers' style as "a plantation atmosphere."[4]

In addition to racial discrimination, Sterling has had two sexual harassment lawsuits by women who worked for him and one to ward off a palimony suit.

Sterling's reputation clearly is tarnished. *Sporting News, The New York Times*, and *Forbes* described Sterling as "one of the worst owners in sports. He even heckled his own players."[5] In fact, Sterling's fall from power may well be his legacy. In a new poll, he was voted the most hated man in America, leading Bernie Madoff and O.J. Simpson.

If Sterling had been a slave owner in a past life, which is likely, then his discriminatory behavior would have been publicly accepted in another lifetime. Fortunately, such attitudes are no longer acceptable, as evidenced by the NBA's decision to ban Sterling. At least now, whether or not Sterling has learned any lessons, he was a catalyst for Americans to rise up publicly against racism. And past-life believers can examine Sterling's present-day patterns as revealing his possible plantation owner past.

Chapter 10

* * *

Johnny Depp

Famous for his role as a pirate wearing roguish hats, scarves, and garish jewelry, Johnny Depp is the highest paid actor in the industry, having earned $75 million in 2012. And, his *Pirates of the Caribbean* series has even turned into a franchise for him.

From the beginning of his career, Depp decided to appear only in films that felt right for him, and Depp clearly loves flamboyant, whimsical, yet conniving characters such as Captain Jack Sparrow. In fact, Depp identifies Sparrow as his favorite role. Depp loves the character: "Captain Sparrow is definitely a big part of me."[1]

Maybe Depp is right on—maybe Depp was a pirate in a past life?

Depp embraced the character of Captain Jack Sparrow so deeply that for the first *Pirates of the Caribbean* movie, he wanted some of his teeth to be gold-capped. He apparently capped too many, and the Disney boss told him to remove most of them. Depp also donned two skull rings: one to remind him that life is short and another to remind him to live each moment to the fullest.

Depp not only relates to the lost-soul quality in the character, but revels in the magic when a kid tells him he loves Captain Sparrow.[2] He clearly connects to pirates. Depp has played Sparrow in four *Pirates of the Caribbean* installments, which have earned him more than 10 award nominations, including both Academy and Golden Globe nods.

Depp performs Sparrow so well, it's difficult to tell where the character ends and the actor begins. In real life, Depp has a tattoo on his right forearm of a sparrow flying over water with the word "Jack," his son's name, inscribed under it. Even the swordmaster for another of Depp's roles said that Depp's ability to wield a sword was as good as you can get.[3] How come performing a pirate and wielding a sword is so easy for Depp? Has he done it before?

A rebel in his early life, Depp got involved in vandalism, drugs, and cutting himself. At the age of seven, his family moved to Florida from Kentucky. Depp doesn't have a mental picture of the houses they lived in—they lived in more than thirty homes in twelve years. His father worked as a civil engineer; his mother worked as a waitress. Depp says that his mother cursed like a sailor, played cards, and smoked cigarettes. His parents divorced when Depp was fifteen.

Withdrawn and odd, Depp ran with a bad crowd. When he was twelve, his mother gave him a guitar. He found a chord book in a shop and stuffed it down his trousers. Depp taught himself to play and began playing in the garage band, *The Kids*. At thirteen, he stole his mom's crushed velvet shirts with French sleeves and seersucker bell-bottoms. He dreamed of having platform shoes. Even then, he liked flamboyant clothes.

At sixteen, Depp dropped out of high school to become a rock musician and moved to Los Angeles with the band. At twenty, he married a makeup artist, Lori Allison, and to make ends meet, Depp sold ballpoint pens. He fell into acting when his then-wife introduced him to her ex-boyfriend, actor Nicolas Cage. The two divorced in 1985.

Eventually, Depp landed his first legitimate movie role in the horror film *Nightmare on Elm Street*. Three years later, he achieved stardom in the lead role of *21 Jump Street*.

While Depp's career was escalating, his personal life was problematic. He was accused of selling drugs at his club, *The Viper Room*, when River Phoenix died of a drug overdose outside the club. While Depp used drugs and sunk into depression, explosive reports of his relationship with supermodel Kate Moss and their trashed hotel rooms filled tabloids.

While filming *The Ninth Gate* in France, Depp met French actress, singer, and model Vanessa Paradis. Paradis became pregnant with the couple's first child. Three years later, the couple had a son, Jack. Depp says he fell in love the moment he set eyes on Paradis. "I was pretty much a lost cause and she turned that around with her incredible tenderness and understanding."[4] Depp learned French to be able to talk to his girlfriend's parents.

Depp and Paradis were together for fourteen years during which they lived with their children in his house in the French countryside. He would walk to the nearby village for a coffee and no one paid any attention. "I'm just another dad with my daughter on my knee," he said. "Living in France is the first time I can honestly say I feel at home."[5]

The couple broke up in 2012, but Depp owns a vineyard in France and is co-owner of a restaurant in Paris. He believes that France and the rest of Europe have great culture and amazing history and that people there know how to live. Depp may even apply for French, British, or Australian citizenship when he retires from an active movie career.

In early 2015, Depp married actress Amber Heard on a beach on his own private, 45-acre Caribbean island, Little Hall's Pond CayCay in the Bahamas, which is only accessible by boat or seaplane. Depp calls his island "pure and beautiful."[6]

Depp could easily have been a pirate in another life. With a turbulent childhood, perhaps in Britain, he could have become a seaman when he quit school rather than going to Hollywood like he did in this lifetime. As well, there seems to be a pattern in his family life given that this time around his family moved so often, just like ocean drifters, and he describes his mother as "cursing like a sailor."

In his youth, Depp wore his mother's flamboyant clothing, took drugs, and stole. As a telemarketer, he scammed people in sales. He also ran a nightclub. He has a tattoo of his pirate movie on his arm, he wanted gold teeth, and he's an excellent swordsman. Depp's skull rings remind him that life is short. He even owns his own island in the Caribbean.[7]

Depp also loves France so much so that he likely lived in France before with his ex-partner Vanessa Paradis, with whom he claims to have experienced love at first sight. He learned French for Paradis and feels at home there. He may even want to become a French citizen.

With his role as Jack Sparrow, his private island, and his magnetic relationship with French culture, perhaps Depp is tapping back into his roots from other lives.

Chapter 11

* * *

Kim Kardashian &
Kanye West

When the whole world is at your fingertips, it's very significant where you choose to get married. It may even reveal a past life or two in the case of Kim Kardashian and Kanye West.

The 16th century Forte di Belvedere in Florence, Italy, was the romantic site of Kardashian and West's dramatic nuptials in May 2014. The historic site has incredible views of Florence and was designed to protect the city by the Medici family. The location where the fort was placed was considered of strategic importance since the time of Michelangelo; the villa, a luxurious palace, was designed to be the residence of the Grand Duke during times of unrest or epidemic.

Today the area boasts luxurious grounds, and the fortress holds amazing contemporary works of art.[1]

West displayed an aptitude for the arts at an early age. He began writing poetry when he was five years old. West then displayed a passion for drawing and music when he was in the third grade. Growing up in the city of Chicago, West quickly got hooked on hip-hop and started rapping in the third grade. By seventh grade, he was creating, and eventually selling, his musical arrangements. At age thirteen, West wrote a rap song called "Green Eggs and Ham" and convinced his mother to pay $25 an hour to record it in a rough basement studio.

West received a scholarship to attend Chicago's American Academy of Art and took painting classes, but shortly after, transferred to Chicago State University to major in English. At the age of twenty, he dropped out of college to follow his vision of becoming a musician.

West, whose mother was chair of the English Department at Chicago State University, took him at the age of ten to China as part of an exchange program. The only non-native in his class, he quickly learned the language. It's no wonder that the rapper is comfortable travelling internationally.

West says he adores Florence and loves Italy and the Italian lifestyle. The couple traveled to Florence in 2013 incognito and think their daughter North was conceived among Renaissance masterpieces.[2] It sounds quite likely that the West family lived in medieval Italy, perhaps around the time of the Medici family, and that West was a Renaissance artist and musician.

Prior to their exotic wedding in Italy, Kardashian and West invited the wedding party to the historic Palace of Versailles outside Paris. Wedding guests were escorted on a private tour of the grounds and moved into the magnificent, stunning Hall of Mirrors.

The court of Versailles was the center of political power from 1682 until 1789, at the beginning of the French

Revolution. Versailles became the home of the French nobility, the location of the royal court and courtiers. Ambitious courtiers would cluster together in families and alliances. Residents would have access to the king as well as the latest gossip, court drama, and intrigue[3]

Consider the court drama and intrigue Americans watched during O.J. Simpson's murder trial in 1994 when Kardashian's father, Robert, garnered public attention as the primary defense lawyer for the football star. Is it possible that such a role in this life is derived from a past life in the French court?

It would be easy to envision Kardashian, the highest-paid reality television personality, along with her sisters Kourtney and Khloe as well as the rest of the Kardashian family, as members of the French court. This time around, they came to prominence with the reality television series *Keeping Up with the Kardashians.* It's anyone's guess how they came to prominence in Versailles, but past-life believers would likely find it easy to connect such patterns and conclude that the Kardashians had a past life in the high court of France.

After seeing the clothes at court, it's no wonder the Kardashian sisters have launched several clothing collections and cosmetics, while Kim has half a dozen fragrances, reminding us once again of perfumes' origin in France. It's also no surprise, then, that as a bride, Kardashian wore the best in French haute couture, a Givenchy dress to her wedding to West; their daughter North donned a Givenchy look-alike.

West's even been inspired in France. Also a fashion designer, sessions for West's sixth musical solo effort began to take shape in early 2013 in his own personal loft's living room at a Paris hotel.

The newlyweds clearly feel at home in Italy and France. West was passionate about art and music from an early age. As a teen, Kardashian was catapulted into the public eye and is now a well-known fashionista. Both are designers. And, most unusual, they had their wedding celebrations at the historic palace of Versailles and a luxurious, historic fort overlooking Florence. Is all of this a coincidence? Or, is the Kardashian/West deeply held attraction to France and Italy their souls' attempt to return to their European past-life roots?

Chapter 12

* * *

Derek & Julianne Hough

American professional ballroom dancer Derek Hough and his sister Julianne can never remember a time when they weren't dancing. Dancing runs in the Hough genes: their parents met in college when they were both part of a ballroom dancing team, and all four of the Hough's grand-parents were dancers. Inspired by their mother who enrolled them in numerous performing courses, all of the Hough siblings have been acting, singing, and dancing since early childhood. In their youth, they billed themselves as "The Blonde Osmonds."

The siblings began their formal dance training in Utah, and Julianne began dancing competitively at nine. When Julianne was ten, the Hough's parents divorced and sent them to London to train with dance coaches and at the re-nowned Italia Conti Academy of Theatre Arts. There, they trained in all types of dance as well as in singing and theatre performance.

In London, the youngsters created their own pop band when Julianne was twelve; they performed at dance competitions in Britain and the U.S. and showcased their talents in a British television show. At fifteen, Julianne became the youngest dancer, and only American, to win both the Junior and International World Latin Championship. Currently, both Julianne and Derek are world champions of Latin dance.

Derek remained in London for ten years. While there, he acted in several stage productions in London's West End. He then headed for Hollywood and landed on the TV dance-competition series *Dancing with the Stars*.

Derek has won the competition a record five seasons. His winning celebrity partners include model and TV host Brooke Burke (Season 7), Nicole Scherzinger, the lead singer from the Pussycat Dolls (Season 10), actress Jennifer Grey, known for her film role on *Dirty Dancing* (Season 11), country singer and former *American Idol* contestant, Kellie Pickler (Season 16), and *Glee* star Amber Riley (Season 17). Derek is the only pro to have won five of the show's Mirror Ball trophies. He also won an Emmy for Outstanding Choreography in 2013 for three routines that he choreographed on the show.

When Julianne returned to the U.S. at the age of fifteen, she attended high school before heading for Hollywood. She is a two-time professional champion of *Dancing with the Stars* and the youngest professional dancer to win on the program. She won season four with her partner, Olympic gold medal-winning speed skater Apolo Ohno, and then Julianne and her partner, three-time Indianapolis 500 champion Helio Castroneves, became the winners of season five. She also was nominated for an Emmy for Outstanding Choreography.

"Dancing and acting satisfy me in different ways," says Julianne. As an actress, Julianne's first leading role was in the 2011 film remake of *Footloose*. In 2012, she played alongside Tom Cruise in the film version of *Rock of Ages*. Her starring role was in the romantic drama *Safe Haven*, based on the novel by Nicholas Sparks. Julianne says, "Dancing is almost spiritual—you feel free; acting is like free therapy—trying to inspire people.... I always wanted to be like the Hollywood Golden Age actors."[1]

Despite her successes as dancer and actor, Julianne says her ultimate goal has always been a career in country music. As a teen, she knew that if she stayed in London, she'd never be able to try her hand at singing. Although people thought she was crazy to leave her successful dance career in London and start over, she took the plunge. Julianne says, "I've grown up with country music. I love how real everybody is, not just the artists, but the fans."[2] One of her idols is Dolly Parton. The star also likes rhythmic rock music from the 1980s and says that if she had lived then, she would have definitely been going to record stores.[3]

Time would tell that Julianne's choice to branch out was a good one. At the 44th Annual Academy of Country Music Awards, fans picked Julianne as the Top New Artist. With a successful music career added to her list, Julianne has returned to acting. "When I feel like it is the right time, I'll return to my music," she says.[4]

Psychic Edgar Cayce urged us to observe what children do as youngsters. Derek and Julianne Hough were always dancing, not to mention acting and singing, perhaps doing so in a past life during the Hollywood Golden Age. Maybe Julianne feels that she has perfected her dancing and wants to ultimately devote more energy to her singing and acting this lifetime. Perhaps she subconsciously recalls using her singing talents in her last life in the early 1980s.

Cayce also said that it took about 33 lifetimes to develop the skills and talent to become a child prodigy. Clearly, both Derek and Julianne have had many lifetimes as dancers and have probably been a dance team many times. Their many successes in this life would lead past-life believers to conclude that both Derek and Julianne carry dancing in their souls and resonated to it with their earliest memories.

Chapter 13

* * *

Kevin Spacey

Many of us are glued to the Netflix series *House of Cards* to see what Machiavellian endeavors U.S. Democratic Congressman Francis Underwood, played by Kevin Spacey, will employ to rise to Secretary of State, Vice President, and ultimately President. Moment to moment, the ruthlessness of the power-hungry politician continues to shock the senses. Spacey is so believable as the cold-hearted, ruthless pragmatist, that no one would dispute his reputation as a character actor. His believability could point to a past life.

Spacey, an actor, director, screenwriter and producer, grew up in California. His mother was a secretary, and his father a technical writer. As a child, Spacey is said to have been a troublemaker. After setting his sister's tree house on fire, for example, he was sent to military school. He was kicked out after hitting a fellow student on the head with a tire.[1] Was his behavior a precursor for the dark roles he would later become so well equipped to play?

Spacey's interest in acting began at an early age when he would sneak downstairs to watch the late late show on television and then imitate the celebrities he watched. He also began to accumulate a huge amount of information about film, especially in high school when he and his friends skipped school to watch revival films. As a high school senior, Spacey played Captain von Trapp for the school musical, *The Sound of Music*. His early interest in acting is likely a clue to a past life as an actor.

In his early twenties, after a flailing career as a comedian, Spacey relocated to New York City to study drama at Julliard. He also continued performing as a stand-up comic in bowling alley talent contests. To pay bills, he worked as a shoe salesman. He next signed on with the New York Shakespeare Festival and his love affair with theatre began.

Spacey is often typecast as cold-blooded, deceptively clever, and conniving. He received public attention as the beady-eyed villain "Mel Profitt" on the TV series *Wiseguy*. He went on to play a despicable office manager in *Glengarry Glen Ross*, a callous Hollywood boss in *Swimming with Sharks*, and a creepy criminal in *The Usual Suspects*, which won him one of his two Academy Awards. He has also performed roles as an ego-driven district attorney and a serial killer. Along with his overtly sinister roles, Spacey convincingly portrays politicians like Congressman Underwood and a Kennedy-like U.S. senator in a TV appearance of *Crime Story*.

Spacey thinks that several things contribute to someone's "evil" choices. He says, "It's a lifetime of experience and motivations and relationships and terrors..."[2] Again, could this be a past-life theme? On undertaking dark roles, Spacey believes people want his characters to be pure evil. He thinks they're great parts. "These are the parts audiences love to hate. You don't play a villain. You play a person who is doing things they think are quite justified."[3]

In real life, Spacey is anything but dark and sinister. A Democrat, he attended the UK Labour Party Conference with his friend, former U.S. President Bill Clinton. He also travelled to Africa with Clinton to help raise money and awareness for AIDS and economic relief. He has donated $42,000 to Democratic candidates. Spacey also met Venezuelan president Hugo Chavez, co-hosted a Nobel Peace Prize Concert, and joined street protests following the Belarusian president's crackdown on the democratic movement there.

Spacey has been honored by Prince Charles, on behalf of the Queen, for having been artistic director of the Old Vic Theatre in London for ten years. In fact, Spacey said that he intends to take up British citizenship. "I love living in London. I can say with all sincerity that London is my home. There is a part of me that is British now."[4]

Given his acting career and his life, it's easy to visualize Spacey as a theatre actor in London in a past life; it's easy to envision him as a power-hungry statesman in a former life as well.

Chapter 14

* * *

Tom Hanks

By the age of ten, Tom Hanks had experienced "three mothers, five grammar schools and ten houses." Given what he called a "fractured family,"[1] one might label his original career goal to become an astronaut as an escape. As a twelve year old, he was mesmerized by the movie *2001: A Space Odyssey*. He saw the movie in theaters 22 times and each time he found something different. But Hanks says, in the end "he didn't have the math" to be an astronaut.[2]

A geek in high school in Concord, California, who described himself as "shy but flamboyant,"[3] he found his niche in a school drama class. He felt that "theater was as magical a place as existed."[4] Hanks decided to make it his career. After he saw a theater production of *The Iceman Cometh*, he was even more determined to do whatever it took to become an actor.

Hanks majored in theatre arts at Chabot College and began by operating lights and building sets. He began to perform in community theater and eventually made his tumultuous way to New York with his first wife and child. Several years later, he got a deal with ABC on TV's *Bosom Buddies* and moved back to California. He then got a lead in a romantic comedy fantasy movie, *Splash.*

Hanks' career as an actor thrived from that point on. He won two consecutive Oscars for *Philadelphia,* followed by the hit *Forrest Gump.* When he read the script to *Forrest Gump,* he says he was hooked: "I saw it as one of those kind of grand, hopeful movies that the audience can go to and feel ... some hope for their lot and their position in life ... I got that from the movies a hundred million times when I was a kid. I still do."[5]

In his next role as astronaut and commander, Jim Lovell, in *Apollo 13,* Hanks achieved his childhood dream of becoming an astronaut. He even has an asteroid named after him.

Continuing his connection with space, Hanks co-directed the Emmy-Award winning HBO docu-drama *From the Earth to the Moon,* detailing the space program from its inception to the moon landings. Hanks is a member of the National Space Society and a supporter of NASA's manned space program. The Space Foundation recognized Hanks for raising public awareness of space programs.

Besides an emphasis on space, Hanks' career is interlaced with an emphasis on war, particularly World War II.

Saving Private Ryan was a riveting, bloody portrayal of war-torn France after D-Day, and Hanks' attempts to bring back a Native American soldier who was a code reader. The film gained recognition as one of the finest war films ever made. For *Saving Private Ryan,* Hanks received the Distinguished Public Service Award, the U. S. Navy's highest civilian honor.

He was also inducted as an honorary member of the United States Army Rangers Hall of Fame, the first actor to receive such an honor. Hanks was recognized for his accurate portrayal of a captain in the movie, for serving as the national spokesperson for the World War II Memorial Campaign, for being the honorary chairperson of the D-Day Museum Capital Campaign, and for his role in writing and producing the Emmy Award-winning miniseries, *Band of Brothers*. Hanks was also a producer of the HBO miniseries *The Pacific*, a companion piece to *Band of Brothers*.

In addition, he appeared in both the television special *America: A Tribute to Heroes* and the documentary *Rescued From the Closet*. As well, Hanks read excerpts from World War II-era columns for the Burns' 2007 documentary film, *The War*.

Along with his acting work associated with World War II, Hanks also starred in *Charlie Wilson's War* in which he played Democratic Texas Congressman Charles Wilson who arranges for Israeli weapons to be transferred to Afghans so that they can fight the Russians.

Indeed, through film and television, Hanks has become intimately involved in the space program and the history of war, particularly World War II, from the American perspective. He describes himself as a lay historian by nature. "I seek out an empirical reflection of what truth is. I want dates and motivations, and I want the whole story," Hanks says.[6]

Perhaps Hanks was a pilot in another life and appreciates the advancements of conquering space today. He could also have been in the Navy or crewed on ships, given his mishaps with being shipwrecked in three movies and captured by pirates once.

As noted above, in *Saving Private Ryan*, Hanks was tasked with saving a code reader. Maybe as a pilot, his own past life was saved due to spy codes and typewriters. Could that be why Hanks has collected more than 80 manual typewriters from all over the world?

Or maybe he was a war correspondent for the Allies during World War II. That might explain why he would want to tell the American war heroes' story. If he was a past-life reporter in one or more lifetimes, Hanks might well describe history as he does today. Hanks says, "Maybe all human history is truly that connection from person to person, event to event, and idea to idea."[7]

Chapter 15

***

Gary Sinise

The son of a film editor, Gary Sinise was born in Blue Island, Illinois. His family later moved to Highland Park, where he attended high school. A rebel with little interest in school, Sinise focused his attention on playing in bands. As a lark, he and his friends tried out for *West Side Story*. He became hooked on acting for life and credits his love of theatre to his drama teacher.

At eighteen, Sinise and two friends founded the Steppenwolf Theatre Company in a church basement in Chicago. The company became quite successful and continues to this day as an award-winning theatre company.

In addition to acting in several plays at Steppenwolf, Sinise directed some of the theatre's most noteworthy productions, including Sam Shepard's *True West*. The company made its off-Broadway debut with that production, starring

Sinise and John Malkovich, and its Broadway debut with *The Grapes of Wrath* at the Cort Theatre. Sinise is married to actress Moira Harris, an original member of Steppenwolf Theatre. They have three children.

Sinise's Hollywood career began in 1986 when he directed two episodes of the TV series *Crime Story*, followed by *Miles from Home*, starring Richard Gere. His first feature film as an actor was the World War II fable *A Midnight Clear*. He starred in the blockbuster miniseries *The Stand*, followed by his performance as "Lt. Dan" in *Forrest Gump* with Tom Hanks. Sinise's portrayal of the emotionally-and physically-crippled veteran earned him an Oscar nomination and worldwide recognition.

Sinise once again teamed up with Tom Hanks in *Apollo 13*, then starred in the HBO film *Truman*, which earned him the Golden Globe, and *George Wallace*, for which he won an Emmy. In 2000, Sinise appeared in the drama *Mission to Mars* and the thriller *Imposter*. He returned to TV in 2004 to star in the crime series *CSI: New York*.

Sinise was also executive producer of the Iraq War documentary *Brothers at War*. The film features an American military family and the experiences of three brothers. As well, he narrated the highly acclaimed *World War II in HD* as well as the World War II documentary *Missions That Changed The War*.

Of all his performances, *Forrest Gump* is said to be for Sinise the film that started a life's work with the real-life military, especially wounded warriors, who embraces Sinise's disabled and depressed Lt. Dan character as their own. Military servicemen and women relate to his role on a deep emotional level. "Wherever I go for the military, they always call me Lt. Dan. They just can't help it," he says.[1] With his heartfelt connection, Sinise is committed to supporting, honoring, and uplifting military veterans.

After several USO handshake tours in 2003, Sinise formed The Lt. Dan Band, which has played for over 500,000 troops and their families at home and abroad. His endless work on behalf of those who have served has earned him many awards including the Presidential Citizens Medal. Sinise is only the third actor ever to receive this award. Recently, Sinise was named an honorary Chief Petty Officer by the U.S. Navy. He has narrated Army and Army Reserve recruitment ads and is also the National Spokesperson for the American Veterans Disabled for Life Memorial.

For nine years, he has co-hosted the National Memorial Day Concert from Washington, D.C. He never misses because he knows how important it is to keep awareness up for all the sacrifices that are made to maintain our freedom.

In 2011, Sinise launched his foundation, the Gary Sinise Foundation. The flagship project was a custom Smart Home building project for severely wounded veterans. Another project is a "Get Skills to Work" program that helps veterans translate their military skills into advanced manufacturing jobs while empowering employers with tools to recruit and mentor veterans.[2] His foundation has taken on such a priority that Sinise doesn't foresee himself acting again for a while. "It's very full-time for me with the military support work and the Foundation work."[3]

With Paramount's re-release of *Forest Gump* for its twentieth anniversary, more Americans likely will look to Lt. Dan as a reminder of compassion, honor, and service to our returning military heroes as they make their challenging reentry into society.

Sinese is aware that casualties of war extend beyond veterans and beyond the U.S., as evidenced by his co-founding of Operation Iraqi Children. Sinise said, "Iraq is in the news every day, and most of it is bad. But there are some positive stories. And how our soldiers are rebuilding schools and helping kids is one of them."[3]

Clearly, Sinise was impacted by his role as Lt. Dan as much as military servicemen and women have been impacted by his portrayal. This doesn't leave much doubt that Sinise was a, perhaps wounded, veteran of a former War. Could it have been World War II? The Civil War? Both? Since he most often plays a Southerner, perhaps he was a Confederate soldier in a former lifetime. Regardless of which war, Sinise's soul seems to remember the ravages of war, both on the people left behind, like the Iraqi children, and those who return home to mend themselves.

Chapter 16

* * *

Meryl Davis

2014 was quite a year for Meryl Davis. Not only did she win the title of Olympic champion for ice dancing with her partner, Charlie White, but she also was the winner of Season 18 of *Dancing with the Stars* with her partner, Maksim Chmerkovskiy.

Davis began ice skating at five on a local lake in her hometown in Michigan. Five years later, she teamed up with White to dance competitively. They are currently the longest-lasting American ice dance team. They are the first American ice dancers to win the World title, as well as the first Americans to win the Olympic ice dancing gold medal. The pair holds the world record for the short dance, free dance, and total combined score.

Both Davis and White were born in Royal Oak, Michigan, ten minutes away from each other. Their parents are best friends. "We grew up together and know each other so well," says Davis.[1] In their first season together, they won the silver medal at the Junior Olympics in the Juvenile division. The next season, they qualified for the 2001 U.S. Championships. The following season they won the silver medal as novices. Both attend the University of Michigan, where Davis majors in cultural anthropology and White studies political science.

Davis' Dancing *with the Stars* partner, Maksim Chmerkovskiy, has been a professional dancer on *Dancing with the Stars* for fourteen seasons, and he enjoyed his first Mirror Ball Trophy as number one winner with partner Davis.

Chmerkovskiy began dancing at the age of four. Though he broke his right leg in a childhood skiing accident, "Maks" proved his doctors, who predicted that he would never have a career in dance, wrong. He recovered, and six months later, even with a titanium rod in his leg, Chmerkovskiy returned to dancing. Eventually, he became a professional Latin Ballroom dancer.

Chmerkovskiy, whose brother is also a champion dancer, owns five social and competitive dance studios in the greater New York City area and one in Los Angeles. He is one of the creators of a non-profit educational organization dedicated to recruiting, supporting, and training future DanceSport participants.

Following the raw chemistry and passion that Chmerkovskiy and Davis exhibited during their steamy televised dance performances, rumors abounded about whether the pair was dating. Chmerkovskiy's brother is said to believe that they are soul mates. A very private person, Davis called her connection to Chmerkovskiy an amazing relationship. "Our chemistry definitely stems from our friendship and the time we spent together on and off the dance floor," she said.[2]

Her ice partner, White, however, says the pair's steamy connection is just part of the performance. He explains that dance partners have to create the appearance of a romantic relationship. "You want people to believe you are an actual couple."[3] Perhaps he's right; for, both sets of partners have successfully projected that image.

Whether it's purely for performance sake or not, it's quite likely that Davis has partnered with both Chmerkovskiy and White as dancers in past lives, either on or off the ice, and perhaps then, the chemistry was more than showmanship.

Chapter 17

* * *

Clint Eastwood

As an actor, Clint Eastwood is identified as the rough, masculine loner who starred in westerns.

As a youngster, Eastwood played the piano, boogie-woogie style, and wanted to earn a degree in music after high school. He ended up graduating from a technical school in Oakland, California, however, and worked odd jobs as a hay bailer, logger, truck driver, and steel-furnace stoker.

In his early twenties, Eastwood was drafted into the U.S. Army and based at Fort Ord in Monterey, California. While in the Army, an actor he met convinced him to take a screen test in Los Angeles. After he finished his military duty, he signed a contract with Universal Studios for 75 dollars a week. His rugged looks eventually landed him on the TV series *Rawhide*, which ran for eight seasons.

Eastwood became internationally known when he went to Italy to star in three "spaghetti westerns: *A Fistful Of Dollars, For a Few Dollars More* and *The Good, the Bad and the Ugly.* In all three westerns, he wore the same poncho without ever washing it.

Eastwood's career eventually shifted back to a string of American-made western movies in which he's played drifters and deputies. He is said to be able to handle pistols with either hand, and he even learned to mountain climb for one role.

Eastwood describes Westerns "as a period gone by, the pioneer, the loner operating by himself, without benefit of society...he takes care of the vengeance himself.... It's the last masculine frontier... a man was alone, on horseback..."[1] He modernized the western marshal role into the modern-day tough police inspector in what became his *Dirty Harry* series. His portrayal of Harry Callahan elevated Eastwood to super-star status.

Eastwood revisited the western genre in the self-directed film *Unforgiven,* in which he played an aging ex-gunfighter long past his prime. It garnered him an Oscar for Best Director as well as a nomination for Best Actor. Interestingly, in the film he wore the same boots he had worn in the TV series *Rawhide.* They are now part of his private collection, having book-ended his career in the Western genre. Eastwood is an avid collector of western art.

Another successful role for Eastwood was the romantic movie, *The Bridges of Madison County.* In it, Eastwood plays Kincaid, a lonely individual... "a lost soul in mid-America." "When I was doing it, I said to myself, 'This romantic stuff is really tough. I can't wait to get back to shooting and killing.'"[2]

While others see him as comfortable in his Western roles—Eastwood has actually had people come up and ask him to autograph their guns—surprisingly, Eastwood has never considered himself a cowboy. "But," he says, "when I got into cowboy gear, I looked enough like one to convince people that I was."[3] The contrast with *"Madison County* allowed Eastwood to appreciate how at home he really felt in westerns.

In addition to his numerous acting roles, beginning with the thriller *Play Misty for Me,* Eastwood has directed over thirty films, including Westerns, action films, and dramas. For his work in the films *Unforgiven* and *Million Dollar Baby,* Eastwood won Academy Awards for Best Director and Producer of the Best Picture, and received nominations for Best Actor. "My involvement goes deeper than acting or directing. I love every aspect of the creation of motion pictures and I'm committed to it for life," he says.[4]

One of Eastwood's latest directorial films is *Jersey Boys,* based on the musical about the Four Seasons. Another is the biopic war drama *American Sniper,* which received six Academy Award nominations and won one for Best Sound Editing. His directing style has been described as "shoot first and act afterwards."[5] Such an approach sounds like a carry-over reaction from a life as a cowboy.

Eastwood has gotten to incorporate his musical abilities in his films. He has composed more than seven film scores and received two Golden Globe nominations for the music in *Grace Is Gone.* Fulfilling a childhood goal, he was awarded an honorary Doctor of Music degree from the Berklee College of Music. Is it possible that Eastwood could have developed his love of music while a lonesome cowpoke with only a guitar for company around his past-life campfires?

Eastwood is rugged and an individualist. He says, "There's a rebel lying deep in my soul. Anytime anybody tells me the trend is such and such, I go the opposite direction. I hate the idea of trends. I hate imitation; I have a reverence for individuality."[6]

Perhaps that loner cowboy was also a business entrepreneur during the Industrial Revolution--having a vision and loving every aspect of seeing his ideas being created into reality. Some of his directorial, leadership, and organizational skills may have been developed in a life such as this. Eastwood has also been involved in politics. After having been sworn in as a California Parks Commissioner, he held up his new badge and told the crowd, "You're all under arrest."[7] As past-life believers know, what one jokes about could be a clue to a former lifetime.

Even his political role as elected mayor of Carmel, California, could be indicative of a past life. Is Eastwood harkening back to his western roles and past lifetimes as the marshal of a small Western town?

Chapter 18

* * *

Jennifer Lopez

"The Supernova" was Jennifer Lopez's nickname growing up in the Bronx. It's a perfect representation of everything Lopez is—a pure expression of her vitality, energy, talent, and star quality. Born in a modest Bronx apartment to Puerto Rican parents, Lopez is the middle of three girls. To keep them off the streets, her parents encouraged the three young Lopez sisters to do performances in the living room. By the time she was five years old, Lopez was being schooled in singing and dancing. Two years later, she toured New York with her school.

Lopez went to a girl's Catholic school where she did gymnastics, played softball and tennis, and competed in national track championships. As a youngster, she was already planning what types of music she would incorporate into her own style. Lopez says, "I was in third grade when 'Rapper's

Delight' changed my life. But, when I came home, my mother would be listening to Celia Cruz, Tito Puente, Diana Ross. I wanted to include all those elements in my music."[1]

Although she loved music, the film industry also intrigued Lopez. Her biggest influence was the musical, *West Side Story*. While a senior in High School, she got a role in a low-budget film, which inspired her to become a "famous movie star." Her parents discouraged her, telling Lopez it was a "really stupid" idea and that "no Latinos did that."[2]

Lopez moved out, worked in a law office, took dance classes at night and slept in the studio. She began performing in stage musicals and music videos. After she won a national dance competition, she became one of the dancing "Fly Girls" on the TV series *In Living Color*.

Exuding star quality, Lopez took the film industry by storm when she beat out 11,000 competitors and was hired to star as the Latino singer Selena, who was murdered by a fan. Even Selena's father approved of Lopez portraying his daughter. The performance ignited Lopez's re-connection with her Latin roots. For her stellar performance, she was nominated for a Golden Globe award and later became the highest-paid Latina actress in history, her salary: $1 million.

Lopez's musical career also began to take off, as she released her debut album on the heels of her successful hit single, "If You Had My Love." It went platinum within two weeks, making Lopez an icon of Latin cultural influence in pop music.

Nicknamed by her fans, Lopez changed her name to J. Lo. When her album, *J. Lo* debuted at No. 1 on the pop charts, her film, the romantic comedy *The Wedding Planner*, shot to the top at the box office. Then, the release of the record *This Is Me ... Then* concurrent with a starring role in the box office hit *Maid in Manhattan* was another double-win for Lopez.

Both the industry and the public were fascinated by the multi-talented Lopez, who had transitioned from a TV dancer to a film star to a pop star, and even a sex symbol, wearing scantily-clad costumes and revealing runway dresses, such as the exotic Green silk Versace dress Lopez wore down the red carpet at the 2000 Grammy Awards. The neckline plunged several inches below her navel. The image was downloaded a half-million times in 24 hours.

Even though her career skyrocketed, Lopez's personal life has been rocky. She has had three marriages and three serious relationships. She is the mother of twins, who made $6 million for their one-month-old baby pictures for the cover of *People Magazine.*

Not afraid of hard work and having learned a strong work ethic from her parents, Lopez continues to add to her awe-inspiring resume. She has been a celebrity judge on American idol for several seasons. As the good business magnate that she is, Lopez has a fashion and home collection line and a perfume line. She has also represented Fiat and Chrysler in promotions. As for charities, Lopez is a strong supporter of L.A's Children's Hospital and the American Red Cross.

Lopez also is a role model and political lobbyist for more Hispanic diversity on television and in other facets of life. "There's a big revolution going on, it's like a media and cultural revolution of Latinos here in the United States. We're realizing our power. We're realizing that we matter here," she says.[3] Lopez is stepping up to her role as a model for Latino self-empowerment, which may indicate that she has experienced more than one life as a Latina.

All her life, Lopez identified herself as a singer and a dancer. "I always wanted to be an actress. For me, it's all just one thing," she says.[4] It seems that on a soul level, Lopez recalled having been a dancer, singer, and performer in other lives—perhaps she was a salsa and tango dancer in South America or a flamenco dancer in Spain. Perhaps she was a Vegas showgirl, or a saloon girl, who enjoyed wearing revealing costumes and exuding a sexy image. Perhaps Lopez was even a harem girl who belly-danced seductively. Whatever the case may be, Lopez clearly carries in her soul the confidence to demonstrate her talents in public.

If you were eighteen and growing up in the Bronx, would you believe your parents if they told you your dreams were impossible, especially for a Latino? Lopez must have trusted on a soul level that being famous was her destiny. She never quit and never stopped believing. That inner conviction coupled with her talent and confidence from other performing lives helped her beat out 11,000 competitors to star in the movie role of her life, one that would allow Lopez to realize all her larger-than-life dreams.

And, because her destiny is stardom, decision makers intuitively recognized Lopez's "star quality," which might actually be the energy surrounding the truth of her stepping into her rightful role as a famous acting, singing, and dancing star during this lifetime.

Chapter 19

* * *

Reese Witherspoon

It's no stretch to imagine actress Reese Witherspoon, a blond, refined, beauty-contest winning debutante as a Southern Belle on a plantation during the "Old South." The well-mannered, optimistic, super-achiever appears to an onlooker as a carbon copy of the polite, sorority sister, Elle (L) Woods, in the award-winning movie, *Legally Blonde*.

Witherspoon was born in New Orleans. Her father was a military surgeon, and her mother was a registered nurse who later earned a Ph.D. in pediatric nursing. Witherspoon spent the first four years of her life in Germany. The family then relocated to Nashville, Tennessee.

As a child, Witherspoon was in gymnastics and considered herself "a big dork who read loads of books."[1] At the age of seven, she appeared in her local Sunday newspaper modeling kids' clothing. She also started children's acting classes at a community college. By nine, she was taking adult acting classes. By eleven, she took first place in the Ten-State Talent Fair. Witherspoon attended an all-girls' school where she was a cheerleader. Once, as extra credit for a high school class, she worked as an office production assistant for a film. After graduation, she attended Stanford University as an English literature major but left after one year to pursue an acting career.

By then, she was no stranger to acting. At fifteen, Witherspoon landed her first lead role in a feature film as a tomboy in *The Man in the Moon*, which earned her rave reviews. Critic Roger Ebert commented, "Her first kiss is one of the most perfect little scenes I've ever seen in a movie."[2]

By 22, Witherspoon was a rising Hollywood starlet, especially after she earned a Golden Globe nomination for her role of a competitive, ambitious over-achiever in *Election*.

Her role as aspiring law student Elle Woods in the comedy *Legally Blonde* placed Witherspoon on the A-list. While making *Legally Blonde 2*, she said, "I had 50 outfit changes. I'm into this whole "girlie" thing."[3] A sorority girl with brains who achieves goals through goodwill is not a stretch for Witherspoon. In fact, she is often cast as upbeat women convinced of their own success. "I grew up in an environment where women accomplished a lot," she says.[4]

But she also likes challenging, complex roles. For example, Witherspoon starred in *Vanity Fair*, a 19th century period piece about a Londoner whose poor childhood makes her determined to find fortune. Witherspoon's character had a child in the movie, and coincidentally during filming, Witherspoon was pregnant with her second child. She felt it enhanced her role: "the fleshiness and ample bosom."[5] The *Los Angeles Times* identified the role as "a part Reese Witherspoon was born to play."[6] As a side note, Witherspoon collects old embroidery, and many fashionable ladies of that time embroidered. Perhaps she was born to play that role because she lived that role in a previous life. That is, perhaps since Witherspoon suited the role so well, was pregnant at the same time as the character's pregnancy, and collects embroidery, she lived in 19th century England as a woman climbing the social ladder.

Witherspoon has performed many roles, and some, like her role in *Vanity Fair,* seem so well suited to her. In 2006, she took home the best actress Oscar for her role as June Carter Cash in the Johnny Cash biopic *Walk the Line,* another role that was equally well suited to Witherspoon. Interestingly, Witherspoon had previously played June Carter's mom, Mother Maybelle Carter, in her 4th grade play. And, after singing in the film in front of audiences, a few record companies approached her to record music.

Post Oscar, Witherspoon had a run of roles she dubbed her "love triangle period" including the 1930s circus drama *Water for Elephants,* as a glamorous performer who did stunts on a horse and an elephant.[7] Her gymnastics came in handy in her training for the role. Perhaps she had a lifetime performing in the circus, thus she was able to draw from that lifetime when applying her gymnastic skills for this role.

Some of Witherspoon's other roles include the pregnant wife of a bombing suspect; the mother of one of three young murder victims; a teenage girl with a boyfriend who turns out to be a violent psychopath; a poor girl living in Los Angeles, who encounters a freeway serial killer; a critically ill young girl; and a South African girl who must cross over 1,000 miles of the Kalahari. In *Wild,* which she produced and for which she earned an Academy Award nomination, Witherspoon plays a recovering heroin addict who hikes California's Pacific Crest Trail alone while coping with her mother's death and her own existence.

Perhaps there's a link between some of the serious roles she's played of women and children as victims and her active involvement in children's and women's advocacy organizations. Like some of her roles, Witherspoon, who is interested in reading psychology, may have had some past lives as a female victim or child victim.

Perhaps this is also why she is such a strong advocate of women empowering themselves. "My grandmother was one of the biggest inspirations in my life. She taught me how to be a real woman, to have strength and self respect, and to never give those things away," she said.[8]

Finally, the actress, producer, and wife of talent agent Jim Toth and mother of three, enjoys spreading humor. "There's something timeless and important about making people laugh... Life is hard. It's nice to go escape...If I can give people a movie about hope, love and the future, then I've done my job."[9]

Witherspoon has more than done her job—as both a comedic and dramatic actress in this life and other lifetimes, she is someone who has shown us a life of a struggling woman and mother. Witherspoon has also shown us the refined side of life, harkening back to her Southern Belle lifetime. In all she does, Witherspoon reveals her indomitable strength of character, spirit, and positive mental attitude, which shines through her work, her eyes, and her volunteerism. She does it with the wisdom that past-life believers would suggest that she has accumulated from many lifetimes.

Chapter 20

* * *

Angelina Jolie

Who would have guessed that Angelina Jolie, the woman many identify as the most beautiful woman in the world, wanted to be a funeral director when she grew up. The glamorous movie star is full of surprises. Instead of seeing the stunning woman that she is, she sees herself as "still just a punk kid with tattoos at heart."[1] In school, she was teased for wearing glasses, braces, and being skinny.

As a rebellious teen, she wore black and was more interested in daggers than dresses. "Girlish attractions held no allure," she says.[2] Jolie collected knives. She felt that cutting herself made her feel more alive. She thought about the concept of death and was interested in mortuary science. She took heroin.

Jolie was fascinated with blood, and years later at her first wedding to actor Johnny Lee Miller, Jolie wrote his name in her blood on the back of her shirt. She and her second husband, actor Billy Bob Thornton, wore each other's blood in vials around their necks. "Some people think a big diamond is really pretty," she said. "My husband's blood is the most beautiful thing in the world to me."[3] They signed their wills in blood, and for their first-anniversary, Jolie bought Thornton their cemetery plots in his native Louisiana.

Growing up, Jolie's friends were all boys. By fourteen, she had a live-in boyfriend. When her relationship fell apart, she committed herself to acting. The craft was no stranger to her; her family was in the industry. Her mother, French actress and model Marcheline Bertrand, studied with Lee Strasberg. Her father, Oscar-winning actor, Jon Voight had Jolie join him on screen when she was five years old.

But it wasn't the family's involvement in film as much as her movie watching with her mother that attracted Jolie to the film industry. At eleven, she began studying at the Lee Strasberg Theatre Institute and acted in several plays. At sixteen, she took up modeling as well as a home-study course on embalming. She went on to study film at New York University and later worked with the distinguished Met Theatre Group in Los Angeles.

After several of her early roles in music videos, on TV, and in film, Jolie's acting career sky-rocketed after she won a Golden Globe and received an Emmy nomination for her performance as Cornelia Wallace, the second wife of the Alabama Governor in TNT's *George Wallace*. She also was widely recognized for her lead role as supermodel Gia Carangi, who was addicted to heroin and died of AIDS. For her role in the HBO miniseries, she garnered another Golden Globe. Then, she earned the Academy Award for her role as a sociopathic mental patient in *Girl, Interrupted*.

Jolie became an international superstar as Laura Croft in *Tomb Raider*. She took the role because she liked the challenge of preparing for it physically. She liked the firearms

and hand-to-hand combat, the martial arts, the dog sled-
ding. Interestingly, she did her own stunts. Also, Jolie had
to learn to speak with an English accent. One reviewer commented, "Angelina Jolie was born to play Laura Croft."[4]

Besides the action-spy role in the Laura Croft series, Jolie
has played a secret assassin in a comedy opposite her husband, Brad Pitt, the neglected wife of a CIA officer in *The
Good Shepherd,* and a CIA agent in *Salt.* Past-life believers
might sense a trend here.

Recently, as a writer and director, Jolie made her directorial debut *In the Land of Blood and Honey,* a love story between
a Serb soldier and a Bosnian prisoner of war, set during the
Bosnian War. Her second directorial venture, *Unbroken,* is a
film about the World War II hero Lou Zamperini, a former
Olympic track star who survived a plane crash in a life raft
only to get to land to spend two years in a Japanese pris-
oner-of-war camp. While filming, Jolie enjoyed coffee and
talks with Zamperini many mornings. She says these talks
impacted her.

Aside from her acting and directing, Jolie has adopted
three orphans: Maddox from Cambodia, Pax Thien from
Vietnam, and Zahara from Ethiopia. With Brad Pitt, Jolie
birthed daughter Chivan in Namibia and twins, Knox and
Vivienne, in Nice, France.

Interestingly, Jolie says she that she adopted her son
Maddox from Cambodia because she feels so connected to
that country. While on location there, she visited a refugee
camp, which she described as a "sea of misery." She said,
"When I met suffering people, it put my life into perspective. It slammed me into a bigger picture of the world."[5] Her
experience led her to begin her humanitarian campaign,
visiting refugee camps all over the world. Because of her
compassionate connection to Cambodia, she believes that
she was a Buddhist abbot at the world's largest Buddhist temple, Angor Wat, in a past life.[6]

If so, she has carried over her compassion from that life-time as a monk into her charitable work now. Besides vis-iting refugee camps, she is well known as a UN Goodwill ambassador who fights for the rights of women and children the world over. She donated $1 million in response to an international emergency appeal in Pakistan. In Western Kenya, she and Pitt fund a compound that includes schools, roads, and a soy milk factory. Jolie has built at least ten other schools in Cambodia, and funds a care facility for children affected by HIV in both Phnom Penh and Addis Ababa. She has also built girls' schools in Kenya and Afghanistan.

Involved in child and women protection efforts, Jolie pushes for legislation to aid child refugees and is fronting a campaign to end sexual violence in war zones by investigat-ing and prosecuting perpetrators of war rape.

With this myriad of past-life puzzle pieces, from all over the globe, and from death and blood to acting, it seems ex-tremely likely that Jolie was a spy, perhaps in Nazi Germany, or a Freedom fighter in France. Not surprisingly, she and Pitt own a home in France and Jolie birthed their twins there.

Perhaps she saw the atrocities of women being raped and children abused. She witnessed the tattoos of the Jews be-ing sent to the camps, the starvation and the inhumanity of their bodies being dumped in pits. Is that why she wears tattoos now and is so thin? Why she likes weapons? No won-der, then, this lifetime Jolie places importance on a proper burial by a funeral director and gave her former husband, Thornton, a funeral plot as a gift

Perhaps if she had witnessed the seamier sides of the Holocaust and other wars, she better understands death. "There's something about death that's comforting. The thought that you could die tomorrow, frees you up to appre-ciate life now."[7] As a believer in past lives, Jolie is hopeful about the possibilities of reincarnation and has a different perspective on death and rebirth.

In addition to a past life during which Jolie witnessed war and death, perhaps Jolie was tortured with a knife and had to play mind games to retain some control. Perhaps, this past life is a source of her fascination with blood. As well, perhaps she saw children torn from their families and orphaned. This lifetime she could do something about some of those inequities. She could adopt orphans and supply others with schooling, health care, and homes. Jolie clearly responds in this lifetime to experiences she carries in her soul from past lifetimes and seems to be fulfilling her greater soul mission.

She uses her public image to speak out on rape during war and uses her ability as a director to select films that make an impact on viewers' psyches in relation to the horrors of war. Of the World War II movie *Unbroken*, she says "to teach my kids something about life, it's better just to show them."[7]

In all, as the U.N Special Envoy, Jolie speaks out about crimes against humanity. In real life, she is the tough, empowered, and beautiful Laura Croft who beats the bad guys. She also plays and directs others in those roles. Perhaps Jolie was more right than she thought when she said, "Therapy. I don't need therapy. The roles I choose are my therapy."[9] Her family and her Good Will humanitarian work are also her therapy.

Jolie has beautifully blended the insights she's gained about war with the empathy learned in her past life as a Buddhist monk and is using her life as an actress, mother, wife and director to help raise the consciousness of the world.

Chapter 21

* * *

Brad Pitt

More powerful than a mere mortal, Brad Pitt embodied Achilles in the epic-film *Troy*. For the role, he gained more than twenty pounds of muscle and practiced swordsmanship for weeks. Ironically, he hurt his Achilles tendon while on set, and the film had to be delayed.

This bigger-than-life figure was born to a mother who was a school counselor and a father who ran a trucking company. Pitt lived most of his early life in Springfield, Missouri, which he described as "Mark Twain country, Jesses James country."[1] Even as a six-year-old choirboy, Pitt got attention because his face was so expressive.

In high school, Pitt was on the golf, swimming, and tennis teams, and performed in a few musicals. In college, he did some acting at fraternity shows. Two credits shy of graduating with a journalism degree from the University of

Missouri, Pitt moved to Los Angeles to pursue acting. There, he took acting lessons and worked odd jobs. He loved films: "they are a portal into different worlds for me," he said.[2] Pitt supported himself by chauffeuring strippers in limos and moving refrigerators.

After years of supporting roles, Pitt first gained recognition as a sexy cowboy hitchhiker in the road movie *Thelma and Louise*. Later, he earned his first Golden Globe nomination for his role in *Legends of the Fall*, which was set in the American West. In 2007, Pitt portrayed the American outlaw Jesses James, the man who defined, for Pitt, the area where he had grown up. Pitt's roles could be indicative of a possible past life as a cowboy in America's West.

Speaking with an Irish brogue from across the pond, Pitt, as an IRA terrorist and later as an Irish gypsy boxer, was barely understandable because his accent was so convincing. Was his language ability carried into this life from an Irish lifetime?

In completely different roles, Pitt twice has performed as a spy, once as a CIA operative in the thriller *Spy Game* and then as an assassin in the action comedy *Mr. and Mrs. Smith*, where he fell in love with co-star Angelina Jolie.

As for World War II movies, Pitt played an American resistance fighter battling Nazis in German-occupied France in *Inglourious Basterds*. In his latest World War II film, *Fury*, Pitt plays a U.S. Army sergeant who commands a Sherman tank called "Fury" and its five-man crew on a deadly mission behind enemy lines.

Pitt, who is a pilot in this life as is his partner, Angelina Jolie, could have been a resistance fighter in France in World War II or an Allied Pilot. The fact that Pitt and Jolie own a home in France and that their twins were born there, could indicate that they lived there, or had been there, in a previous life. Perhaps that's why they were drawn to buy a chateau and birth their twins there.

Pitt, who has an attraction to architecture, did an in-formal apprenticeship with a renowned architect in his Los Angeles office. Pitt says he'd like to design something like a city or museum. Carrying this interest into TV, he narrated a PBS television series focused on building environmentally friendly structures through sustainable architecture and de-sign. He also contributed money by starting a foundation to finance and construct 150 sustainable, affordable new houses in New Orleans following the devastation caused by Hurricane Katrina. Pitt says, "I want to do something with my hands other than just play golf."[3] It sounds like Pitt was an architect in another life but doesn't have time to pursue those interests in depth in this life.

Pitt's roles as actor, producer, designer, and activist are coupled with his role as husband and father, all of which keep him quite busy. Who we marry often provides a signifi-cant clue into a past life. For Pitt, it is fascinating that in 1997 Pitt appeared in the war biopic drama *Seven Years in Tibet* as Austrian mountaineer Heinrich Harrer, who became a tutor and friend of the young 14th Dalai Lama. Pitt's wife Jolie be-lieves that she was a Buddhist monk in a past life. Given Pitt's role as Harrer and his attraction to Jolie in this lifetime, it's likely that Pitt, too, was a Buddhist before.

And then there's his possible life as Achilles, or some major ancient Greek general. Serendipitously, Jolie played the cold-blooded mother of Alexander the Great in another historic epic. Jolie, who had pet snakes growing up, and a tattoo snaking up her arm, seems to understand and own the role of a mother of a powerful, epic general and the dangers that entails. She could have been Pitt's mother or lover in another lifetime.

Overall, it's relatively easy to decipher Pitt's past lives as a cowboy, an Irishman, a World War II resistance fighter in France, and an architect. He's surely also been a Buddhist and an epic general. Finally, past-life believers couldn't disagree that Pitt and Jolie have loved one another again and again throughout their lives.

Chapter 22

* * *

Leonardo DiCaprio

At the age of fifteen, Robert De Niro picked Leonardo DiCaprio out of near obscurity and from 400 young actors to play the lead role in *This Boy's Life*. During auditions, De Niro had been intimidating the youngsters to see if they would stand up to him. When his turn came, DiCaprio screamed in De Niro's face. The rest is history. This role put DiCaprio on the big screen, and he demonstrated that he could hold his own next to De Niro and perform as a serious actor.

DiCaprio was named after Leonardo da Vinci because his pregnant mother was looking at a Leonardo da Vinci painting in a museum in Italy when DiCaprio first kicked. His mother was born in Germany and was a legal secretary when she met DiCaprio's father, George, at college. George was a comic book artist who distributed cult comic books.

DiCaprio's parents divorced when he was a one year old. While a youth, he lived in Germany periodically with his mother's parents and learned to speak German. In the states, DiCaprio and his mother lived in dangerous areas of Los Angeles, places inhabited with prostitutes and drug dealers. DiCaprio got beat up. His dad, a hippie, would take him to parades where they marched as Mudmen in their underwear, carrying sticks and covered with mud.[1] Not motivated, DiCaprio dropped out of high school before senior year.

From an early age, the only thing DiCaprio knew for sure was that he wanted to be an actor. At five, he was taken off the *Romper Room* TV set for misbehaving. "The earliest memories I have are jumping onstage before concerts in downtown Los Angeles and trying to get on the mic and break-dance, or be a comic in class," he said.[2] One of his passions was to meet people, imitate them, and create different characters. He also liked doing his own homemade skits. As a youngster, his parents got him an agent who suggested he change his name. He didn't. DiCaprio's career began with his appearance in several commercials and educational films. As a teen, he landed a role in the sitcom *Growing Pains*.

After his breakthrough movie with De Niro, DiCaprio co-starred as the mentally challenged brother of Johnny Depp's character in *What's Eating Gilbert Grape*, the story of an unbalanced farmbelt family. A critic noted, "DiCaprio made his character's many tics so startling and vivid that at first he was difficult to watch."[3] At nineteen, he became one of the youngest actors to be nominated for an Academy Award for Best Supporting Actor.

While only 22, he returned to De Niro's side, starring in *Marvin's Room*, with Meryl Streep and Diane Keaton. DiCaprio portrayed Streep's troubled son, who was committed to a mental asylum for setting her home on fire.

To advance his career, DiCaprio paid his own way twice to Australia to lobby for the lead role in *Romeo and Juliet* opposite Claire Danes. The investment paid off. He became an instant worldwide heartthrob.

With his tough roles, DiCaprio proved he was more than a pretty face. His acting style is intense, patterned after his mentor and role models Robert De Niro and Jack Nicholson. In fact, he often plays tortured souls dealing with their past, men who have suffered loss or trauma, or those who are ultimately unfortunate. Take his ill-fated role in *Titanic*, the highest-grossing film to date, assuring his role as an international heartthrob.

He's also more recently known for his role in *Catch Me If You Can* as the ill-fated teen Frank Abagnale, who fakes three careers as a Pan Am pilot, assistant district attorney, and physician to make millions writing bad checks. Not unlike the real DiCaprio, who came from humble beginnings, Abagnale used his charm, confidence, and wits to create a totally new reality of success. Both DiCaprio and Abagnale also were very connected to their mothers.

Upping the ante in his next role as Jay Gatsby in the film *The Great Gatsby*, DiCaprio was smooth and elegant but vulnerable. He reveals his humble background and his cover-up in high society. Although he makes his money illegally, he does so to win his first love. Roger Ebert suggested this role as DiCaprio's best performance.

Playing a much more eccentric character, DiCaprio has also paired up with Martin Scorsese to portray aviation pioneer Howard Hughes in *The Aviator*. DiCaprio reportedly spent more than eighteen months preparing for the film. In a TV interview, he revealed that the role brought back his own obsessive-compulsive disorder that he had exhibited as a child.[4] This personal identification could have left a special bond with and compassion for the tortured character of Hughes.

From troubled tycoon to twisted tycoon, in *The Wolf of Wall Street*, DiCaprio played stockbroker, Jordan Belfort, who was arrested in the late 1990s for securities fraud and money laundering. Although DiCaprio's early life on the rough side of the tracks taught him not to make destructive life choices like drugs and prostitution, that exposure allowed him to understand and portray the callous nature of greed.

The winsome DiCaprio has played a variety of roles. His roles have ranged from heartthrob to eccentric. But from his earliest memories, he wanted to be an actor. As a child, he played at entertaining, a past-life clue. As a teen, he became one of the youngest actors to be nominated for an Academy Award. How could he excel so young without any training? Yet another past-life clue. These clues point to another lifetime as a performer.

By the time he was 22, he had acted with Robert De Niro twice and starred with Meryl Streep and Diane Keaton. Had he known these mega-actors and actresses in a past life?

Synchronicity, a meaningful experience outside yourself, seems to have helped his acting career. De Niro picked him out of 400 boys for a lead in a movie. When DiCaprio's role in a western was dubious, Sharon Stone paid his salary. In another movie, he replaced River Phoenix who had died during pre-production. He paid his way to Australia twice to lobby for a role that propelled his career forward. So, DiCaprio got some lucky breaks. These "breaks" could be another clue to an acting past life.

Even the themes that run through his career roles may resonate with his life, and perhaps other past lives as well—characters who deal with their demons and their pasts. Maybe underneath the smooth, refined exterior of DiCaprio's handsome persona, is the boy who grew up defending himself in fights in a rough area, or, with the early rejections of a highly competitive career, doubting his own acting abilities and continuously challenging himself to be better.

Maybe one reason DiCaprio can play complex personalities so well is that he taps into the part of his soul where he remembers pain or differences from a past life. Maybe he is drawing on a depth of past experiences of hard living to bring to the surface intense emotions and hard edges. Perhaps, for example, his soul recalls struggling to feed his family as an Irish immigrant or fighting for his turf, not unlike his character, the leader of a 19th century Irish gang in *Gangs of New York*. But DiCaprio turns these cellular memories into advantages. "You can either be a vain movie star or try to shed some light on different aspects of the human condition," he said.[5]

Most probably, DiCaprio has drawn on his own loss or trauma from a past life. Perhaps the loss of a wife or loved one might make DiCaprio hesitant of making a commitment to marry. "I don't know if I'm ever getting married. I'm probably not going to...unless I live with somebody for ten or twenty years...We don't have the guts that Romeo did," he said.[6]

He often plays misguided magnates (*The Aviator, The Great Gatsby, Django Unchained,* and *The Wolf of Wall Street*.) In this life, DiCaprio has risen from humble beginnings to one of the biggest movie stars in the world who makes $20 million a movie. Perhaps in another lifetime, such as during the Industrial Revolution, DiCaprio was a tycoon who had risen from poverty.

In this lifetime, DiCaprio, a movie star mogul, shares his successes; he is using his money and energy as a committed environmentalist and humanitarian. DiCaprio has been appointed as a United Nations representative on climate change. He has donated $1,000,000 to earthquake relief and $1,000,000 to the Wildlife Conservation Society.

DiCaprio likes to help the whales and dolphins as well. The first place he heads for a break from acting is the sea. In one of his early films, *The Beach*, he played an American backpacker searching out an idyllic secret island commune off Thailand. The actor must have had some happy or peaceful memories in a lifetime by or on the sea.

With Di Caprio's career as an actor and director still evolving, it will be fascinating to observe more past-life clues as they unfold in the movies and the humanitarian work he chooses in the future.

Chapter 23

* * *

Helen Mirren

It is paradoxical that British actress Helen Mirren, who considers her upbringing to have been very anti-monarchist, would achieve international recognition for playing a queen six times, including both Queen Elizabeth I and Queen Elizabeth II, and the wife of King George III. She has won 29 major awards, including an Academy Award for her portrayal of Queen Elizabeth II in *The Queen* and Olivier's Award for Best Actress as Queen Elizabeth II in the play, *The Audition*. She has been honored with the title of "Dame" for her contributions to the performing arts.

Mirren's father played the viola with the Philharmonic Orchestra and later drove a cab before becoming a government worker. Her mother came from a large London-based family and was the granddaughter of the butcher to Queen Victoria. Mirren's other grandfather, a White Russian diplomat, got stranded in London during the Russian Revolution and had also become a taxi driver to support his family.

From the age of six, Mirren wanted to become an actress in the "old fashioned and traditional sense." She grew up in a world without TV and never went to the movies. At thirteen, she saw an amateur production of *Hamlet*. "I was blown away by this over-the-top drama. All I wanted was to get back into that world where all those fabulous things were possible."[1]

Against her parents' wishes, she began acting in high school and continued at London's New College of Speech and Drama. By twenty, she played Cleopatra at the Old Vic and soon became a member of the Royal Shakespeare Company, performing scores of classics. Her stage career thrived. The single-minded, sexy, often bawdy vixen made it to Broadway and earned Tony nominations.

Branching out into film, Mirren was willing to take unconventional roles. Her roles ran the gamut from playing Hitchcock's wife to a retired Israeli operative and from comedic roles to the mother of a Belfast prison hunger striker.

On the television screen, Mirren's hard-nosed detective persona in *Prime Suspect* kept viewers hooked for seven seasons. And, on the BBC 16th century historical miniseries *Elizabeth I*, Mirren exhibited a range of strength, femininity, and humanity in portraying the British monarch.

Clearly, Mirren has a grasp on the pulse of all things British, both currently and historically. Maybe her early Shakespeare training has given her some insight. "If you wanted to teach someone who knew absolutely nothing about the British people, it would be very good to guide them to Shakespeare. You see the foolishness, the humor, and the brutality. It's all in almost every play."[2]

So, what past-life clues does Mirren exhibit? First, she has had a love of acting since the age of six and a deepening passion for acting that intrinsically has interwoven itself into Mirren's life and artistic expression beginning in high school. Her incredible talent has been recognized in every venue. If there are past lives, Mirren has acted in other times, perhaps even in Shakespeare's time.

Even though Mirren grew up in a working class home, she is able to be believable as a queen, particularly a British queen. She does not cower as a mere mortal but takes up the mantle of power and the regal nature of her roles. The fact that she has been cast as a queen six times, on stage, in film, and on television in a miniseries, is indicative of a variety of casting directors visualizing Mirren embodying the role.

Like the Virgin Queen, in this life Mirren has never wanted children. "I was never going to be anyone's mum or grandmother. But I can dig...feeding the masses."[3] It is apparent that Mirren is driven by her artistic passions and that's where her priorities lie. "I am so happy that I didn't have children...because I've had freedom."[4] These attitudes, priority of focus, and her believability in these roles could indicate that Mirren was British royalty in one or more lifetimes.

In *The Debt*, Mirren was a tough Mossad operative tasked with capturing a Nazi war criminal, who had conducted medical experiments on Jews, and returning him to Israel. For her role, Mirren immersed herself in studies of Hebrew language, Jewish history, and Holocaust writing. Couple this with the fact that her Tsarist grandfather was an aristocrat who was in London negotiating an arms deal during World War I. Ironically, Mirren has chosen to take political action by bringing attention to the proliferation of illegal small arms throughout the world, which Mirren believes, is causing such devastation. Perhaps Mirren was a spy in another lifetime in World War I or even during the Holocaust.

In her personal life, Mirren married her partner, director Taylor Hackford, in a rented castle near Inverness, Scotland.

Hackford, an American of Scottish descent, wore a traditional Scottish tartan kilt.[5] A Scottish past life together is likely. Mirren and her husband relax in their 500-year-old medieval castle in southern Italy. It is complete with turrets. Although it has proven to be a restoration nightmare, perhaps it triggers happy memories of another possible past life together in 6th century Italy. More royal European lifetimes? The couple used to own an estate in New Orleans. Although they sold it, New Orleans remains Mirren's favorite American city. Her interest in this specific geographical area hints at a New Orleans lifetime as well as her lifetimes in Europe.

Another past-life telltale sign is the tattoo of a star Mirren has on her left hand. It was acquired at a Native American reservation in Minnesota and is an American Indian symbol meaning "equal but opposite." Her tattoo suggests a Native American past life in addition to her past lives of European royalty.

An acclaimed English actress, Mirren describes herself as quite spiritual. She may believe in fairies and leprechauns.[6] Perhaps some of these past-life clues will help her trigger deeper, in depth past-life memories upon which she can draw in her creative work and in her understanding of her life, her love, and her multidimensional self.

Chapter 24

* * *

Ben Affleck &
Jennifer Garner

B en Affleck was raised in Cambridge, Massachusetts largely by his mother, Chris, a public elementary school teacher who had been educated at Radcliffe College and Harvard University and had been a Mississippi freedom rider in the 1960s. As a child, Affleck and his brother Casey were encouraged to make their own home movies. Since their mother had friends who were performers, she regularly took them to the theater. Affleck has had acting jobs since the age of seven.

When he was eight, he met what would be his life-long friend and colleague, ten-year-old Matt Damon, who lived two blocks away. Their mothers, both divorced school teachers, encouraged the friendship.

Affleck's father, an actor who had worked with some
big names, also did odd jobs ranging from bookie and bar-
tender to a janitor at Harvard University. His son later co-
wrote with Damon the janitor role into the script of *Good Will
Hunting*. After what he referred to as "some scary and trying
episodes" due to his father's alcoholism, Affleck's parents divorced when he was eleven.[1]

Wanting to be an actor ever since he can remember,
Affleck got a role in a Burger King commercial and on an
HBO film because his mother was a friend of the casting di-
rector. Affleck acknowledged that he had "chanced into it."[2]
As a teen, he appeared in TV movies, including one in Mexico
to where he travelled and learned Spanish for the job.

Best friends and little league teammates, Affleck and
Damon spent their high school lunch hours mapping out
their acting careers. They were inspired by their drama
teacher and saved money to go to New York together for auditions. Early on, they were hired to star in a T.J. Maxx commercial together. Later, the pair would share apartments in
the Hollywood area as they strove to climb the film ladder.
They blew through what they thought was a fortune, $35,000
each before taxes, from their earnings in *School Ties*, and had
to leave their Venice apartment.

After a series of indie films, Affleck finally felt he had
a good role, when his director friend Kevin Smith wrote
Chasing Amy with him in mind. He lived on the director's
couch during the filming.

But Affleck's career, dovetailing with his best friend
Damon's, was propelled into the national limelight and star-
dom when the pair, age 25 and 27, won the Oscar for the Best
Original Screenplay, *Good Will Hunting*. This breakthrough
role allowed Affleck to choose roles in blockbusters such as
Armageddon and *Pearl Harbor*.

As a naval officer in *Pearl Harbor*, he first met his future
wife, Jennifer Garner, who played a nurse. At the time,

Affleck and Garner were both involved with others, and Garner wasn't in Affleck's playing field.

Garner had her own rise to stardom with her role as a college student/CIA operative in the TV thriller series *Alias*, which ran for five years. To prepare for the audition, she took private Taekwondo lessons to learn how to throw a punch and kick. For her role, she was nominated for four Emmys, four Golden Globes, and two Screen Actors Guild Awards.

By the time Garner was cast as Affleck's love interest in the spy movie *Daredevil*, he came to her rescue when she got tangled in some wires. As she came crashing towards a wall, she recalls "out of nowhere comes this 6-feet-4-inch red devil who puts his arms out and shouts: 'I've got her!' It was like, 'I've got my own superhero.'"[3] By the time the pair was in *Electra* together, she really did get her man. Even though Affleck's scene was ultimately cut, the pair fell in love while filming. They were married in 2005 and have three children.

All told, Affleck has portrayed three superheroes and worn both the Batman and Superman suits. He is planning another return as Batman and had the lead in the thriller *Gone Girl*.

Fifteen years after his first Oscar, Affleck won his second, directing *Argo*. *Los Angeles Times* critic Kenneth Turan recognized Affleck's talent as a director and acknowledged Affleck's "instinct for storytelling."[4] Affleck agreed that *Argo* was a power story. "*Argo* demonstrates the power of storytelling, whether it's political theatre...or trying to get people out of danger.... The camera can be more powerful than the gun," says Affleck.[5] A true story, *Argo* portrayed the CIA escape of American prisoners from Tehran who pretended to be filming a sci-fi movie there in order to get out of the country. It is noteworthy that, prior to his involvement in *Argo*, Affleck learned to speak Arabic and majored in Middle East affairs in college.

So, looking at this snapshot of Affleck, what past-life clues can we glean? First, he was a child actor and focused on his acting career incessantly. Was he an actor before? It seems likely. In addition, Affleck likely has been a writer in the past, as well as an owner of a company who not only has a vision but also can direct and manage others to achieve that vision.

As husband and wife team, Affleck and Garner described as "down-to- earth," have acted in three movies together; the first was *Pearl Harbor* in which Affleck was a naval captain and Garner was a nurse. Both actors could have been in World War II together. Ironically, Affleck has a fear of flying in this lifetime. Maybe he subliminally remembers the bombing in Pearl Harbor or was a pilot who's plane was shot down. During a USO tour in the Persian Gulf, Affleck visited troops stationed there. He is now involved in two charities that support the troops.

The pair also has acted as CIA operatives—Affleck in *Argo* and Garner in the TV series *Alias*. Garner has even hosted a CIA recruiting video. Were they spies in a former lifetime? It's likely. Both have also portrayed superheroes. Maybe they have been instrumental in helping society by fighting "bad guys."

On his own, with his interest in learning Arabic and Middle Eastern studies, attending the star-studded opening of Dubai's lavish Atlantis Palms resort, and acting and directing in *Argo*, it appears that Affleck has had a lifetime in the Middle East, whether as a Middle Easterner or a foreign diplomat.

An avid poker player, Affleck has been tutored by professionals. In 2004, he won the first prize of $356,400 at a California State Poker Championship. Affleck has noted that he thinks it's fun both to do the math and to use his intuition to read people. Affleck could be a natural because he was a gambler, on a riverboat, or elsewhere, before.

Besides having had past lives with his wife Garner, it's clear that Affleck has lived past lives with his best friend and colleague, Damon. Thirty years later, Ben and Matt are still best friends. Affleck finds it grounding to have a friend he's been connected to since he was a little kid. "Matt and my brother Casey are the two people I rely on the most, emotionally and professionally," he says.[6] Their families have vacationed together. For several years, they have been living near each other in Los Angeles. "I've been hounding him to live here so our kids can know each other, go to the same schools and hang out the way we did," Affleck says.[7] Apparently, he not only wants to nurture his friendship, which may have lasted over several lifetimes, but also wants to afford the next generation of Afflecks and Damons the blessings of friendship that their parents have shared.

Chapter 25

* * *

George Clooney

Growing up in a family of well-known media personalities and movie stars, George Clooney's first role on TV at five years old was playing sketch characters on talk shows that his dad hosted. Nick Clooney, a former anchorman and game show host, was the brother of singer Rosemary Clooney. Rosemary's husband was Academy Award winner José Ferrer. George's mother Nina was a former beauty pageant queen.

Raised in Kentucky and Ohio with his older sister Ada, the Clooney kids were sent to Catholic schools and had a strict upbringing. Clooney was an altar boy. In Clooney's first year of high school, he developed Bell's palsy and half of his face was paralyzed for nine months. He turned his attention to sports. At sixteen, he tried out for the Cincinnati Reds but didn't make the cut.

At night around the supper table, the Clooney family would discuss the latest news. Clooney decided to major in Broadcast Journalism at Northern Kentucky University but never graduated. He didn't want to be compared to his father. He drifted through jobs from selling women's shoes and doing construction to picking tobacco. When his cousin Miguel Ferrer offered him a small part in a feature film, Clooney refocused on acting and moved to Hollywood. Slowly, parts came in.

Clooney's first major break was as an orderly in the medical sitcom *E/R*. Ten years later, it would take another medical TV series, *ER*, to launch him as a superstar. This time he was lady's man and pediatrician Doug Ross, MD. While simultaneously acting in movies that ranged from romances to war dramas to superhero stories like *Batman*, Clooney continued to wear his TV scrubs for five years.

When Clooney did turn in his scrubs, he did so to focus not only on acting on the big screen but also on producing and directing films. So far, Clooney's biggest commercial success is his *Ocean's Eleven trilogy*. In addition to the trilogy, the actor has been in six heist-robbery movies. His characters are often likeable scoundrels or gangsters.

Along with his heist films, Clooney has also been involved in a number of war dramas. He starred in two Persian Gulf War dramas, *Three Kings* and *The Thin Red Line*. His movie, *The Monuments Men*, focused on a team of Allies tasked with saving Europe's priceless art treasures from Hitler. Past-life believers might equate his involvement in war dramas in this life as a clue to his past. If Clooney had a past life in World War II, however, it may not have been an experience that led to shell shock and trauma.

His production of *Argo*, a true diplomatic coup by a CIA operative who saves the lives of American diplomats, garnered Clooney an Academy Award for Best Picture. He also won an Academy Award for Best Supporting Actor for his production of the Middle East thriller *Syriana.* In his role, Clooney, a CIA agent, witnesses petrochemical politics and the international influence of Persian Gulf oil. Clooney's CIA performances do not stop there. Additionally, Clooney directed a spy comedy film, *Confessions of a Dangerous Mind,* about Gong Show host Chuck Barris, who claims to have been a CIA assassin.

In the political arena, Clooney runs for president in *The Ides of March,* which he co-wrote and directed. He also directed, co-wrote, and acted in *Good Night and Good Luck,* a film about the conflict between veteran broadcast journalist Edward R. Murrow and U. S. Senator Joseph McCarthy's anti-communist investigations.

All told, Clooney has earned three Golden Globes and two Academy Awards, one for acting and the other for producing. He's the only person ever to be nominated for Academy Awards in six categories.

As for his activism in politics and humanitarianism, Clooney was appointed a U.N. "Messenger of Peace" in 2008. He's been an advocate for the Darfur conflict and organized a telethon to raise money for Haitian earthquake victims. With his father, he was arrested at a staged protest at the Sudanese embassy in Washington, D.C. In 2012, Clooney raised $15 million in contributions for President Barack Obama's re-election campaign.

In 2003, Clooney, an early opponent of the Iraq War, told a German TV reporter "America's policies frustrate me."[1] While some have wondered if Clooney would shift to political office, Clooney claims he won't run. "I've slept with too many women, done too many drugs, been to too many parties," he explained.[2] Because he cares so deeply about international crises and the human condition, however, people still speculate whether he will run for office.

Clooney's father ran, unsuccessfully, for Congress, and in *The Ides of March,* which he co-wrote and directed, Clooney's character runs for president. Perhaps Clooney was a politician in another lifetime. Perhaps he found that he couldn't accomplish as much as he wished through the system. Now, perhaps, he realizes that he may make a more valuable global contribution as a movie star and a filmmaker. Maybe that's one reason why he is so drawn to films that reflect his liberal political beliefs.

As a celebrity and filmmaker, he says, "I don't make policy, but I can shine a light on faulty or good policy. We need to focus global attention on the plight of 2.5 million civilians who have fled their homes..."[3] As for the Academy, he says "We're the ones who talked about AIDS when it was just being whispered. And we talked about civil rights when it wasn't really popular...I'm proud to be a part of ...this community."[4]

From an insider's view of governmental politics and international affairs, Clooney's movies explore covert activities. He has directed several biographical CIA dramas and played the role of a CIA operative. Perhaps, if Clooney was a CIA spy in a past life, he would be more apt to challenge authority and the governmental status quo during this lifetime. He might experience frustration when observing the slow-moving wheels of government and the untimely resolution of issues and crises because he has more directly been involved in them in a past life.

Another of Clooney's possible past lives associated with politics could have been as a news reporter. After all, Clooney's major in college was broadcast journalism. His father was a news anchor. He directed, co-wrote and acted in the story of famed broadcast journalist Edward R. Murrow.

On a lighter note, Clooney may have been a good-natured con-man, white collar scoundrel, or gangster since he's played nine roles, including his biggest commercial success, his *Ocean's Eleven trilogy*, in that capacity.

In another lifetime, Clooney also could have been a professional athlete. In high school, he loved to play basketball and baseball. Although he tried out for the Cincinnati Reds, he didn't make the cut this time around. Nonetheless, it's likely he's excelled as an athlete in a past life.

Finally, it is likely that Clooney has been with his wife, Lebanese-born British human rights barrister Amal Alamuddin, in past lives. The fact that one of the world's sexiest stars and most influential of men waited until he was 53 years old to find his wife is indicative of just how special this relationship is. There is no doubt that besides Alamuddin's stunning looks, her intellect and commitment to international and humanitarian goals are important common denominators in their relationship.

The pair met in Italy, married in Venice, and owns a palatial villa overlooking Lake Cuomo. Chances are they knew each other in Italy in a past life. It is also interesting to note that, given Alamuddin's Lebanese ancestry, Clooney directed and acted in several movies based in the Middle East. The couple could have shared a Middle Eastern past life together.

It is fortunate that Clooney, who grew up around fame and, after being sidetracked by life, got nudged back on track to a career as an actor, filmmaker, and political activist. Without wasting time running for political office and dealing with a frustrating political system, Clooney can reach millions of minds and hearts through his films and celebrity status.

About his political movie, *The Ides of March*, he says, "It's not a bad thing to hold a mirror up and look at some of the things we're doing (politically)."[5] In addition to his own sense of fulfillment and happiness, Clooney is using his "celebrity credit card" wisely to help raise the world's consciousness. He has rightfully been dubbed by the United Nations a "Messenger of Peace," and it's clear that he's returned to earth this time to fulfill that destiny.

Chapter 26

* * *

Matt Damon

For Matt Damon, role-playing was therapeutic. His mother was a divorced early childhood education professor in Cambridge, Massachusetts. Along with his brother, they lived in a communal house. As a lonely teenager, he grappled with his self-identity due to his mother's structured approach to child rearing.

His schoolmate Ben Affleck, his tenth cousin, became his friend. Together, they shared their love of drama in high school theatre. They later even shared a Boston bank account, which they used to travel to New York for auditions.

While at Harvard University, Damon skipped classes for his acting projects. When he thought his film role in *Geronimo* would be a success, he dropped out of college, twelve credits short of graduating, and headed for Hollywood. He got his first break with a one-line role in the comedy, *Mystic*

Pizza. Taking his acting seriously, Damon made himself sick by losing forty pounds for his role as a drug-addicted soldier in *Courage*. *The Washington Post* called his performance "impressive."[1]

His career breakthrough came along with Affleck's when, at 27 and 25, Damon and Affleck earned an Oscar and Golden Globe for co-writing their screenplay *Good Will Hunting*. Damon, who played a young math genius, was also nominated for an Academy Award for Best Actor.

His success with *Good Will Hunting* propelled Damon into becoming a Hollywood A-lister. Now, among the top forty of the highest grossing actors, Damon has appeared in three other films nominated for Best Picture: *Saving Private Ryan*, *The Departed*, and *True Grit*.

Among all his roles, Damon is most identified with *The Bourne Trilogy*. His character, Jason Bourne, an amnesiac assassin, is paranoid and on the run. Despite some critics who align the Bourne trilogy with the James Bond films, Damon says there is no comparison between Bourne and the Bond character. He finds the Bond character "repulsive" and calls Bond "an imperialist and misogynist, someone who laughs at killing people...then slugs martinis."[2] In contrast, he describes his character as "antiestablishment, paranoid and on the run." Bourne is not a playboy, but is obsessed with the death of his girlfriend. Damon contrasts the characters further: "He doesn't have the support gadgets and he feels guilty for what he's done."[3]

Another trilogy in which Damon has been involved is the *Ocean's Trilogy*. Damon plays a young thief, who runs with a clever, upscale thieving pack, who represents an updated version of the rat pack. During the filming, Damon bonded with George Clooney and Brad Pitt. The trio played jokes on each other on set.

In 2007, Damon joined the ranks of *People Magazine's* "Sexiest Man Alive," thanks in part to his colleagues, Pitt and

Clooney, who were already in the "club." Damon responded, "you've given an aging suburban dad the ego-boost of a life-time."[4] Damon, also in Clooney's *Monument's Men*, attended Clooney's Venice wedding.

The trio teamed up to found the humanitarian organization "Not On Our Watch" which focuses global attention and resources to prevent mass atrocities, such as those in Darfur. Damon is also involved in fighting AIDS and poverty in third world countries, hunger relief, and bringing safe drinking water to developing areas in Africa.

Along with Affleck and two other producers, Damon also founded "Project Greenlight" to find and fund exceptional projects of neophyte filmmakers.

While acting in Clooney's geopolitical thriller *Syriana* as an energy analyst, Damon learned he had a fear of heights. On a break, he and his wife, Lucy, were watching the sunset over the Arabian Peninsula from the top of an elegant seven-star Dubai hotel. As he walked to the edge, he described his legs locking up. "I was absolutely frozen. I completely jumped my neocortex and went straight to this primal, full lizard brain fear state."[5] Such a reaction or phobia usually indicates a past-life death from heights.

In his personal life, Damon is happily married to Luciana Barroso. Born in Argentina, she met Damon in Miami while she tended bar. For Damon, it was love at first sight. Today, the couple has four daughters, including one from Luciana's previous relationship. Damon's past-life clues are evident in his relationships. His feeling of love at first sight with Barroso indicates he has been with her before.

He's also been with his colleagues Clooney and Pitt in past lives. Whether in the *Ocean Trilogy* or *Monument's Men*, the trio can be humorous while taking life and death risks. Perhaps they were Robin Hood types...robbing the rich to give to the poor. This lifetime, they all give generously to the poor and underprivileged.

They also could have been in the U.S. military together in World War II. *Monument's Men* transpired in World War II. (Although Pitt wasn't in *Monument's Men*, he has played a number of World War II roles, including *Fury* and *Inglorious Basterds*).

As for his life-long friendship with Affleck, Damon definitely has been with him in other lives. From their early beginnings in little league, the co-writers skyrocketed to international success winning the Oscar for *Good Will Hunting*. At lunch in high school, the friends nurtured each other's dreams of acting. It seems likely they were writers and actors together in the past. They grew up living two blocks from each other and now live just miles apart. They share their love of baseball and gambling. Most likely, they shared a gambling lifetime together too, although Affleck seems luckier at the tables this time around.

As for his signature role as Bourne, Damon is a rogue CIA assassin suffering from memory loss. Since he is so identified with this role in the *Bourne Trilogy*, it appears that Damon could have been a past-life CIA operative or a spy. Interestingly, his buddy Clooney plays a CIA operative in *Syriana*.

Colleague Pitt also has played a spy twice, both as a CIA operative in *Spy Game*, and an assassin in *Mr. and Mrs. Smith* with his wife, Angelina Jolie. Jolie became an international superstar as an action-spy in the Laura Croft series. Jolie has also played the neglected wife of a CIA officer in *The Good Shepherd* and a CIA agent in *Salt*.

As for best friend Affleck and his wife Jennifer Garner, the couple have both acted as CIA operatives—Affleck in *Argo* (co-produced by Clooney), and Garner in the TV series *Alias*. Garner has even hosted a CIA recruiting video.

Were they all spies in a former lifetime? It seems likely. Did they work together before? It's entirely possible. Perhaps these colleagues and their wives have become friends, because, in part, they remember trusting each other with their lives in other lifetimes.

And, the plot thickens: perhaps we have identified some "group karma"—a group who has come back together this life to work together and accomplish some like-minded goals. It's obvious by their priorities and actions, that each actor and actress in this esteemed group is helping humanity on a global level. Perhaps in their capacity as directors, producers, writers, and actors, they are selecting and acting in roles that point out a duplicity in government as well as the humanity behind wars and geopolitical issues that affect us today.

This begs the question: Why are spy movies so popular at this time? And, in what other ways will this "movie gang," both collectively and individually, reach out to affect the thinking of the masses?

Chapter 27

* * *

Catherine Zeta-Jones & Michael Douglas

To help focus her abundant energy and because she loved musicals, her mother, a seamstress, and father, owner of a candy store in Swansea, Wales, gave Catherine Zeta-Jones singing and dancing lessons beginning at the age of four. As a child she soon began performing with the local Catholic troupe, and by the time she was ten, she had the lead role in the musical *Annie*. At twelve, Zeta-Jones won recognition as a national tap dance winner in England; she also was performing a production of *Bugsy Malone* in the West End. By that time, her parents agreed to let her move to London with a tutor and perform on stage.

Performing had always been her dream. Zeta-Jones remembers "growing up and wanting to be on stage. I wanted to get to London as soon as possible and start auditioning for theater. My life was my work."[1] By fifteen, she had her first actor's guild card. She also had the lead in the musical *42nd Street*. Growing up in Wales, she had never thought about being in movies. But in the early 1990s, her role as a sexy farm girl in the TV series *The Darling Buds of May* propelled her overnight into one of Britain's most popular TV actresses.

While appearing in the American TV movie *Titanic*, she caught Stephen Spielberg's eye and he cast her in *The Mask of Zorro* with Antonio Banderas. For her role, she studied dancing, riding, sword fighting, and Spanish. She spoke so well that after the movie, people would speak to her in Spanish. Seven years later, she filmed a sequel.

Zeta-Jones' breakthrough role came in *Traffic* for which she earned a Golden Globe nomination for Best Supporting Actress. Established as a talented actress, Zeta-Jones wowed audiences with her singing and dancing talents as well in the film version of the musical *Chicago*. For *Chicago*, she received an Academy Award for Best Supporting Actress and another Golden Globe nod. Zeta-Jones acknowledged that she really wanted that role. "That's like saying did I want to wake up in the morning wanting to breathe!"[2] Zeta-Jones has also been recognized with a Tony for her singing talents in the musical *A Little Night Music*.

The actress, listed five times by *People's Magazine* as "One of the World's Most Beautiful People," was introduced to her husband, Oscar-winning actor and producer Michael Douglas during a private screening of *Zorro* in 1998. She described it as "love at first sight...I really do think it was meant to happen."[3] When Douglas met her, he told her, "I want to have babies with you...When I found out she had the same birthday as me (25 years earlier)-ta dah! When I discovered she loved golf, all my fantasies had come true," he said.[4] The couple have two children together: a son, Dylan, and daughter Carys.

A second-generation success, Douglas's father, Kirk, was a major movie star when Michael was growing up. Although his father discouraged him from getting involved in the film industry, Michael took sensitive roles in direct opposition to his father's macho roles. He has often played successful business executives and political figures, including the American President. Aside from his screen roles, Douglas is known for his political activism: he was named a United Nations Messenger of Peace, and he has helped to focus both worldwide attention on nuclear disarmament and human rights and national attention on handgun control.

Looking at the couple's past-life clues, they both experienced love at first sight while meeting each other. It is a poignant clue in which one or more of the pair seem so attracted to and comfortable with each other at first meeting that it is as if they are picking up right where they left off in another time, with an already developed, often passionate relationship. Douglas thought it was synchronistic that the pair has the same birthday. Synchronicity is another past-life clue.

While both actors seem to have been in love before, both actors also seem to have been actors before. Although his famous actor-father discouraged him, Douglas grew up wanting to act. Douglas, who plays successful businessmen and political roles with believability and has been involved as a political activist, has most likely been a decision maker in past lives, both in the world of business and politics. Just like his recurring roles, you could easily imagine him in executive offices, on the political stump and in the back rooms where behind-the-scenes decisions are made.

As for Zeta-Jones, she's been awarded "Commander of the Order of the British Empire" for her accomplishments in film and television. There can be no mistaking that Zeta-Jones was a performer and entertainer in other lifetimes. She wanted to be on stage from her earliest memories. She was dancing, singing, and entertaining at four. What you do at an early age is a past-life clue. Zeta Jones' fast career track—a lead in a musical at age ten and a national tap dance winner at twelve, would indicate that she had talent beyond her years and experience. Another past-life indicator. There's no doubt the Zeta-Jones was a dancer before. "I was a chorus girl. That's all I ever wanted--to be on stage. I would queue up for auditions and then change my costume...and audition again. It might take me two tries, but I always got the job."[5] It's a sure bet she was a chorus girl in the past, perhaps a vaudeville entertainer, maybe even a Vegas showgirl or dancer for the Follies. Or, maybe she was a nightclub entertainer in Chicago during the roaring twenties.

Zeta-Jones has wished that she was born in the era of "dancing with Fred Astaire and Gene Kelly and going to work at the studio dressed in beautiful pants, head scarves, and sunglasses."[6] Although she was born in 1969, before either dancers died, their early dancing careers were on the stage— Astaire's in Broadway and London, and later, in the glory days of Hollywood in the 1920s, '30s, and '40s, and Kelly's on stage in the '30s and in film in the '40s. It's extremely likely Zeta-Jones shared the stage with the dancing greats—even if as a hoofer in the chorus line.

Along with her past live(s) as a dancer, it's likely Zeta-Jones experienced life in some significant historical eras as well. It's possible she was attracted to the role of Catherine the Great in a TV miniseries because of a past-life connection. The 18th century Russian Empress revitalized and Europeanized Russia and brought in the Golden Age of Russia. Although Zeta-Jones may not have been the Empress in a past life, she may have been a Russian noble at the time. In another historical role, for the musical version of *Spartacus*, she played the Thracian prophetess Palene. Spartacus was a Thracian gladiator and military leader around 100 B.C., who helped lead a slave uprising against the Roman Republic. It is entirely possible that Zeta-Jones held a position of power in the Grecian-Roman culture.

Chapter 28

* * *

Sandra Bullock

The actress often dubbed "America's sweetheart," Sandra Bullock, spent the first twelve years of her life in Germany. Her first language is German. Born to a German opera singer mom and American vocal coach dad, Bullock took singing, piano, and ballet lessons while traveling around Europe for her mother's career. At the age of five, she appeared in a German opera and then began performing in the opera's children's choir in Nuremburg.

Returning to Virginia, the pre-teen was bullied at school for wearing frumpy German clothes, but Bullock got involved in gymnastics and theatre and became popular as a cheerleader. Her classmates christened her "Most Likely to Brighten Your Day."[1] While studying acting at East Carolina University, she was elected Homecoming Princess. With just one class remaining, Bullock left college to pursue acting in New York.

At 21, she received enough attention from her role as a Southern belle in the off-Broadway production, *No Time Flat,* to get an agent and, ultimately, roles in TV and film. Her breakout role in *Speed* made her a star. Bullock was amazed. "Never did I think a bus movie would open every door I possibly wanted to open," she said.[2] In demand, the popular actress has exuded an image of a wholesome girl next door who portrays ordinary women in extraordinary circumstances.

Her roles have ranged from romantic comedies to crime thrillers and more serious dramas. She often plays a detective, cop, or writer, even in comedies, such as her roles as a cop in *Miss Congeniality 1* and *2* and *The Heat* with Melissa McCarthy. Bullock also was a detective in the crime thriller *Murder by Numbers.* And, in *A Time to Kill,* Bullock portrayed a law student who helped resolve a Mississippi court case involving a father on trial for allegedly killing his daughter's rapists. She played the writer Harper Lee in *Infamous,* the story of Truman Capote's investigation of a brutal Midwest massacre. In *28 Days,* Bullock plays a belligerent alcoholic newspaper writer who is sent to rehab.

But it was her 2009 performance as the adopting mother of football player Michael Oher in *Blind Side* that netted Bullock a Golden Globe and an Academy Award for Best Actress. As well, her almost solo role in the critically acclaimed film *Gravity* led to her recognition by *Entertainment Weekly as 2013* Entertainer of the Year—that was her second time earning the title. By 2014, Bullock was reported to be the highest-paid actress in the world.

In her personal life, Bullock has a ranch in Austin, Texas and homes in Jackson Hole, Wyoming and Tybee Island, Georgia. She is the mother of her adopted son Louis. After a five-year marriage, she divorced motorcycle builder Jesse James, former star of the TV hit *Monster Garage.* Some members of the Hell's Angels had been present at their wedding.

The friendly, unpretentious Bullock seems to be the kind of person you could throw in a pool. That's exactly what friends George Clooney and Tom Cruise thought at a birthday party in 2002.[3] To Bullock, fame means, "when your computer modem is broken, the repair guy comes to your house a little faster."[4] When hearing about her 2nd Oscar nomination in 2014, the down-to-earth star was thrilled but, she said, "I still have to get up and make lunch for a little person, and pray—please dear God—that he eats something I put in his lunchbox today."[5]

As far as being a humanitarian, Bullock has donated $1 million to the Red Cross at least four times: most notably in response to the tsunamis in the Indian Ocean, as earthquake relief to Haiti, and to assist a damaged school following Hurricane Katrina.

So, what past-life clues has Bullock's life exhibited? Normally, she is cast as an average woman, not royalty. She looks like she'd feel more at home in jeans than a red carpet dress. "I'm a horrible celebrity," she says. "If I'm out in public, I dress like a pig."[6] Who else would snort on the big screen? You could imagine her on her ranch in Texas or in Jackson Hole in jeans and boots. Although she's allergic, Bullock loves horses. It would seem likely that the girl who spent her early years visiting opera houses in Europe could have been an American cowgirl or rancher in former lives.

If we believe that we choose our parents and circumstances prior to birth, then Bullock's choice of an opera singing mother and early exposure to performing would be an important clue into her past lives. As a child, singing and performing on opera stages in Germany gave Bullock an early love of entertaining. She was also given ballet and piano lessons as a child. It's no wonder she gravitated to theatre in high school and college and committed to it as her career. She has clearly been an actress before.

Her recurring roles as a cop and detective could indicate lifetimes in law enforcement. She could even have been the arm of the law in a small western town. Being a reporter, writer, and lawyer in several movies could indicate that Bullock has been a researcher, academic, or lawyer and writer in the past. In fact, Bullock wrote the screenplay *Making Sandwiches*, which she produced and directed. She also said that, had she not gone into acting, she would have been a romantic novelist.[7] It seems extremely likely that Bullock has been a writer before.

Personality-wise, Bullock seems to have carried over a genuine, natural presence and optimistic attitude from past lives. She has continued to carry her sunny disposition throughout her school years and into her acting. She doesn't seem to take herself and her stardom too seriously. With her personality and ability to relate to everywoman and everyman—and them to her, the Academy Award winner seems assured of as much acting success as she wants.

Chapter 29

* * *

Richard Gere

An accomplished pianist and music writer, actor Richard Gere played several musical instruments and wrote music for productions in high school in Philadelphia. Gere was the second of five children of two parents who were both Mayflower descendants. His mother was a housewife, and his father, an insurance salesman, had originally planned to be a minister. Gere was raised Methodist.

A boy scout and member of the student council, he was on the gymnastics team, the lacrosse team, and the ski team.

He went to the University of Massachusetts, Amherst on a gymnastics scholarship and majored in philosophy and film. After two years, he dropped out to pursue roles in theatre. He ended up in London playing the lead in the musical, *Grease*. While there, he became one of the few Americans to perform with the Young Vic Theatre.

Gere first gained recognition in the film *Looking For Mr. Goodbar* in 1977. He then went on to Broadway, where he was recognized for his portrayal of a gay concentration-camp prisoner in *Bent*. He established himself as a major star in the lead role of *American Gigolo*. Then, with his role as a troubled pilot in training camp who gets involved with townie, Julia Roberts, in *An Officer and a Gentleman*, Gere's star status was confirmed. In 1990, Gere teamed up with Roberts again in the romantic comedy *Pretty Woman* and later, the box office hit, *Runaway Bride*. His other roles in hit films included a defense attorney in *Primal Fear* and a disturbed hedge fund magnate in *Arbitrage*. Gere won a Golden Globe for Best Actor in the film musical, *Chicago*.

Off screen, Gere is well known as a humanitarian, political activist and supporter of Tibet. Although he was raised Methodist, Gere began studying philosophy in college. He became interested in Buddhism in his twenties. When he was 29, after having studied Zen Buddhism for about six years, he travelled to Nepal and met monks and lamas. After meeting the Dalai Lama in Dharamsala, India, he began practicing Tibetan Buddhism. He returns to the Tibetan headquarters often.

For decades, Gere has been a political activist for freeing Tibet and for human rights there. He helped found "Tibet House," which is charged with preserving Tibetan culture. He also supports tribal peoples globally to help them protect their lives, lands and human rights. Gere travelled with a doctor to refugee camps in Central America and spoke out for human rights in Kosovo. He has campaigned for ecological causes and AIDS awareness, particularly in India.

In his personal life, Gere was married twice. The first time was to supermodel Cindy Crawford. In 1993, *People Magazine* named them "Sexiest Couple." With his second wife, model and actress Carey Lowell, Gere has a son, Homer James Jigme. Gere's third name, Jigme, is Tibetan for "fearless." The couple co-owned the Bedford Post Inn in New York, complete with a yoga studio and meditation center.

Gere's past-life clues indicate that he was a musician and composer at an early age. His first major role was in the musical *Grease* in London. He was one of only a few Americans to perform with the Young Vic Theatre. Gere could well have been a musician and composer as well as a theatre actor in England in the past.

As a youngster, Gere also excelled at sports, particularly gymnastics. Perhaps he was a dancer, gymnast, and entertainer in the past. In this lifetime, Gere danced in an award-winning role in *Chicago* and again in *Shall We Dance?* Perhaps he was a hoofer or vaudeville actor in Chicago in the roaring twenties. Maybe he also appeared on the stage or in Hollywood in the '20s or '30s, when movies were big musical theatricals.

In high school, Gere was on the lacrosse team, a sport developed by Native Americans in North America in 1100. The game was characterized by deep spiritual involvement, focusing on the glory of the warrior. Gere is an advocate of tribal people around the world. Perhaps he was a Native American in a prior life and played lacrosse as part of a spiritual ritual.

Gere, whose father wanted to be a minister, chose philosophy as his college major. In his twenties, Gere became interested in Buddhism. This led to a life-long spiritual quest, studying with Buddhist spiritual masters, meeting the Dalai Lama, and fighting for the rights of a free Tibet. There is no doubt that Gere has been a Buddhist in several lifetimes. Perhaps he has lived in Tibet in the past. Maybe he was even a student of the Dalai Lama or one of the other lamas before. He says, "When I am there (Tibet), I am very happy. The Tibetans radiate. They literally send out light. His Holiness (the Dalai Lama) generates love and compassion to every human being."[1]

Richard Gere, who has played romantic leads, medieval knights, and ruthless villains, believes that "there's really one character for every actor. The voyage is to find that one character."[2] Perhaps Gere's one character, or his voyage, revolves around his embracing of Buddhism, Tibet, and the Dalai Lama.

Chapter 30

***

Renée Zellweger

Film star Renée Zellweger didn't see her first movie until college. The town she grew up in, Katy, Texas, was so small that they didn't have cable TV or a movie theater. Her father, a Swiss engineer, and her Norwegian mother, a nurse and midwife, met on a boat to the U.S. following World War II.

Zellweger was active in sports in junior high school: soccer, basketball, baseball, and football. In high school, she was a cheerleader and gymnast and joined the speech team and drama club. A bright student at the University of Texas at Austin, Zellweger majored in Radio, Film and Television and graduated in three years. While taking an acting class, she discovered an aptitude for it. During her time in college, she did a beer commercial, and a beef commercial, and had a two-line role in a horror-comedy that got cut.

Zellweger decided to stay in Texas and audition for movie roles, while cocktail waitressing. She appeared in several movies, and her first major role was with Matthew McConaughey in the horror film *Texas Chainsaw Massacre: The Next Generation.* McConaughey also was in her next film, *Love and a .45.* The pair of roles garnered enough critical attention to motivate Zellweger to move to Hollywood. Her breakout role as the love interest of Tom Cruise in *Jerry Maguire* made her an international star.

From there Zellweger displayed her versatility, moving from a tear jerker in *One True Thing,* where she was a New York magazine writer who puts her life on hold to help her mother through her last phase of cancer, to the comedies *Me, Myself and Irene* and the lead in *Nurse Betty,* for which she earned a Golden Globe.

Despite her myriad roles, many of us still think of the chubby, bumbling, British TV reporter Bridget Jones when we think of Zellweger. Surprisingly, she almost didn't get the role because she was too skinny. She had to quickly gain twenty pounds, learn a British accent, and spend three weeks working undercover in a British publishing company in order to prepare for the role. Her work paid off—she was recognized with her first Oscar nomination.

Zellweger also received accolades for her performance as Roxie Hart in *Chicago.* Although Zellweger had never taken a dance or singing class before, critics were amazed at how good her voice was and how she "danced up a storm" in the hit musical film.[1] Zellweger said she learned by watching co-star Catherine Zeta-Jones and enduring a strenuous ten-month coaching schedule. In her role as Hart, a murderess vaudeville star wannabe, Zellweger received her second Academy Award nomination for Best Actress, as well as a Golden Globe.

Zellweger went on to win an Oscar for her role in the epic Civil War drama *Cold Mountain* in which she played the gritty role of a strong, self-sufficient woman who helps help-lessly-refined Ada (Nicole Kidman) run her Southern farm.

Other roles for Zellweger range from a social worker in a psychological horror film to a former singer suffering from paralysis, and from London spinster children's writer Beatrice Potter to a Texas schoolteacher in 1933. She's por-trayed a Kansas waitress who suffered a nervous breakdown after witnessing her husband's murder and the depression-era wife of Irish heavyweight boxing champ James Braddock. She's also been a promiscuous widow and lover of a town marshal in a small western town in New Mexico in 1882.

With all those roles under her belt, Zellweger also tried her hand at producing. She got involved producing *Miss Potter* because she wanted more creative control over her script. In a second endeavor, Zellweger co-created and ex-ecutive produced a TV series, *Cinnamon Girl*, about the Hollywood scene in the late 1960s. The TV network *Lifetime* declined the pilot.

Unlike some other movie stars, Zellweger never dreamed of being famous. Her goals were more modest. "I never would have been so bold as to dream these things might hap-pen to me," she said. Her goals were to be self-sufficient, learn, travel and "have my eyes opened."[2] She wanted to be challenged and express her creativity. "When I got my job in a bar and could pay for my tuition, go on auditions and sometimes get jobs that I loved, and pay my rent, I knew I'd be alright. That's when my dreams came true, long before the telephone rang and someone said, "Come meet Tom Cruise."[3]

Unlike some other movie stars, Zellweger didn't dedicate her life to fame. She wasn't given singing or dancing lessons as a youngster. Neither parent was in show business. So, it is interesting that Zellweger appeared to stumble on acting in school and found that she had an aptitude for it. It came eas-ily to her. She was a natural. She didn't rush to Hollywood but stayed in Texas and found movie roles. Three years after graduating from college, she had received critical acclaim for her first major role in the *Texas Chainsaw Massacre: The Next Generation.*

Knowledge and talent beyond experience is a past-life clue. Zellweger didn't study acting from the greats. It is amazing that, with no previous training or experience in dancing and singing, she got the nod for an Oscar for her role in *Chicago.* Perhaps she has performed in other lives, maybe as a vaudeville star in the roaring twenties or even a saloon girl in the west. In this lifetime, she was a cocktail waitress at a strip club. In *Appaloosa,* she was a "loose" widow in a small western town in the late 1800s. Coincidence or past-life clue?

In her Oscar-winning role in *Cold Mountain,* Zellweger plays a coarse, unrefined woman who is able to keep a farm going during the Civil War. Against all odds, she is self-sufficient. The believability of the role she played could indicate that she, like many women left behind, struggled to keep their lives going and remain safe amidst the ravages of the Civil War.

Zellweger has taken on other difficult roles where her character has lost control—a former singer who becomes paralyzed, a waitress who has a mental breakdown after her husband is murdered, and a depression-era wife faced with having her children taken away due to abject poverty. In each case, due to circumstances beyond her control, she is helpless and desperate. Usually, she portrays a working-woman—a waitress, social worker, schoolteacher or reporter. Even her roles in comedies can have victim overtones, and audiences are always bewitched by her wistful smile.

In this life, Zellweger's dream was to be self-sufficient—to pay for her education and lifestyle and move toward a career she found creative. Zellweger, the daughter of immigrants, didn't get things handed to her. Since repeat patterns in our lives, or in the case of actresses, their roles, indicate past lives, it looks like Zellweger has had a number of difficult lives of struggle and dependency. The fact that from her own self-sufficiency, she has created a life that far exceeds her wildest dreams indicates that she has let go of a dependent pattern from other times.

Zellweger, who is single, was married for just a few months. She claims, "I'm not single, I'm busy."[3] Perhaps, through the roles she has played, she has helped to release a fear of dependency since she's fought so valiantly to be self-sufficient. Now, perhaps she can meet a mate who can be her partner, and share her happiness and new dreams while letting go of any (past-life) struggles.

Chapter 31

* * *

Matthew McConaughey

Shoveling chicken manure in Australia and reading an inspirational book changed the direction of Matthew McConaughey's life.

Born in Uvalde, Texas to a mother who was a kindergarten teacher and a father who owned an oil pipeline business but had been drafted by the Green Bay Packers, McConaughey lived a privileged life. His parents married each other three times (they divorced each other twice). He attended an affluent high school, had a golf handicap of four, drove a flashy sports car, and was voted "Most Handsome" by his senior class.

Spending a year in Australia as a Rotary exchange student gave McConaughey a new perspective on his lifestyle and his identity. Time for self-reflection, as well as a lack of a charmed lifestyle and a gang to fall back on, made him more independent. Returning home, he attended the University of Texas at Austin intent on going to law school. When he read Og Mandino's motivational book *The Greatest Salesman in the World,* he got the clarity that he really wanted be in film and got the courage to change majors. A fraternity man, he graduated with a degree in Radio-Television-Film after directing short films and doing commercials.

While still in film school, McConaughey got a lucky break when he met a casting director in a bar and was cast in Richard Linklater's *Dazed and Confused.* Three years later, he appeared to be an overnight success after playing a sheriff in *Lone Star* and a lawyer in *A Time to Kill.* Shocked by losing his anonymity so quickly, McConaughey fled to the solitude of Peru's rain forest. A nature meditation, the actor was reminded to live in the moment—a useful coping mechanism on his fast track to fame.

McConaughey's adventure escape became a pattern. After filming *Reign of Fire,* he backpacked in Africa solo for over three weeks, racing camels in the Sahara and floating down the Niger River. Prior to the release of the film *Sahara,* McConaughey promoted it by sailing down the Amazon and trekking to Mali. He even did voiceovers for a Peace Corps ad.

McConaughey admits that he's proud of being a loner. "Nothing beats the feeling of taking off on my own and driving to wherever the roads takes me," he says.[1]

Besides running on the beach with his shirt off in romantic comedies, McConaughey has been cast as a New Age theologian in the science fiction film *Contact,* a World War II submarine lieutenant in *U-57,* a financial executive in *The Wolf of Wall Street,* a firefighter in *Tiptoes,* a gambling protégé in *Two for the Money,* and a head football coach in *We Are Marshall.* In *Interstellar,* McConaughey becomes the ultimate adventurer who journeys through wormholes into other galaxies and time.

In addition to playing a lawyer in *A Time to Kill,* McConaughey played a property attorney in Spielberg's slave epic *Amistad,* East Texas district attorney in *Bernie,* and a criminal defense attorney in *Lincoln Lawyer.* He's been a crime investigator on the HBO TV series *True Detective* and an idealistic reporter in *The Paper Boy.*

After losing enough weight to look sickly for the role of a cowboy diagnosed with AIDS in the film *Dallas Buyer's Club,* McConaughey hit the jackpot—an Academy Award and a Golden Globe for Best Actor.

In his personal life, McConaughey is married to Brazilian model and TV performer Camila Alves. The pair has two sons and a daughter. As a philanthropist, McConaughey started an organization that helps teens lead active lives and make positive choices.

What types of past-life clues has this adventure-seeker exhibited? For one, McConaughey has a connection to the law. McConaughey, who always loved to debate, had originally planned to be a criminal defense attorney. He has portrayed a lawyer four times, has been a criminal investigator in a TV series, and a crime reporter in a movie. Both McConaughey and his casting directors sense his connection to a profession in law. A past-life or two? Probably.

Despite being born a Texan this lifetime, it's clear that McConaughey has lived the Texas life time and time again. McConaughey looks like a Texan cattle rancher. He spends most of his down time on his 1,600-acre ranch in west Texas. He describes his spirit as "Texan." "We're independent... Try to build fences round us and we'll run you out of town," he says.[2] Interestingly, one of his first roles, in *Dazed and Confused,* was set in Austin, Texas, and two of McConaughey's biggest film breaks took place in Texas too. He appeared to be an overnight success after playing a sheriff in *Lone Star* and won an Oscar and Golden Globe for his role as a Dallas cowboy with AIDS. A Texas ranch owner now, coupled with his Texan roles could point to a past life as a rancher, ranch-hand or cowboy.

As for acting, McConaughey got the break actors die for when he casually met a casting director in a Texas bar. The rest was history. Was this a coincidence or was it synchronicity—a meeting that was predestined to happen? Was he meant to be famous because he had been an actor before? Was he placed on a fast track to success? By April 2014, McConaughey had made the list of *Time Magazine's* "Most 100 Influential People in the World." It's likely this isn't his first lifetime in the limelight.

As for adventuring out into the wilderness alone, there's no doubt McConaughey's comfort level and sense of peace point to lifetimes as a lone trapper, cattle ranger, pioneer, or perhaps as an explorer, archaeologist, or astronaut. Perhaps having had some lifetimes living as a loner without a family is why McConaughey, as an eight year old, wanted to be a father.[3]

The combination of the lone traveler who is willing to plumb the depths of himself and a compassionate and loving father and husband can only help enhance McConaughey's future in film. As the ultimate traveler, he can continue to explore new dimensions in his own acting abilities and expand the film industry with his presence.

Chapter 32

* * *

Denzel Washington

If Denzel Washington's mother hadn't sent him to a military academy at fourteen, and if he had not hung out at the local Boys and Girls Club, he may have ended up in the penitentiary like his street buddies.

The middle child, Washington's father was a Pentecostal minister and his mother a beautician and Gospel singer. Seeding a latent interest in acting, Washington observed his father's showmanship and, while working at his mom's beauty shop, began to appreciate the art of storytelling.

When his parents divorced, his mother and male figures at the Boys Club influenced his sense of morality, community involvement, and social responsibility. It was while he worked at a YMCA camp that Washington joined in a staff talent show and his life path changed.

Washington caught the acting bug and appeared in some college productions. After earning his journalism degree from Fordham University, he got a scholarship to the American Conservatory Theatre in San Francisco. He gained critical acclaim in theater, and landed the lead role in his first film *Carbon Copy*, but his big break came when he was cast as Dr. Phillip Chandler in the TV series *St. Elsewhere.*

While he was filming the six-year series, he won as Oscar nod for his supporting role as an anti-apartheid activist in *Cry Freedom.* Two years later, Washington's role in the epic historic Civil War movie *Glory* as a former slave/Union soldier who was whipped for a mistaken escape attempt won him the Best Supporting Actor Award. It was his role in *Malcolm X* that earned Washington his Best Actor Oscar nomination. Washington finally clinched the Best Actor Award with his role as a bad Los Angeles narcotics cop in *Training Day.*

Now a Hollywood A-lister, Washington has played a jazz trumpeter, a convict, a football coach, a lawyer who defends an AIDS client, a private detective, a paralyzed forensics expert, a man in love with an Indian woman, and an alcoholic airline pilot. To prepare for his role as a reporter, he shadowed *Washington Post* reporters for six months; to play a boxer, he trained for a year.

Washington often plays military leaders and law enforcement officers; he has worn a military uniform in at least six films. *A Soldier's Story*, for which Washington won an Obie Award on stage and later played in the film version, explores discrimination in the U.S. Army in 1944. In addition, he played a disillusioned British soldier and a Civil War soldier. Washington also portrayed two Gulf War soldiers suffering post-traumatic stress. For *Courage Under Fire*, he prepared by being involved in war games, listening to tapes of tank battles in Desert Storm and qualifying on the M1A1 tank and the 120mm gun at Fort Irwin in California. Washington also has visited recovering troops at Brook Army Medical Center in San Antonio, Texas where he subsequently made a large donation to a house used as a hotel for the veterans' visiting families.

As for his police, detective, and forensic roles, it is interesting that, as a youngster, the Boys and Girls Club awarded Washington the title of "Police Chief for a Day." In some films, he has also performed his own hand-to-hand fighting.

In his personal life, Washington is married to actress Pauletta Pearson and the couple has four children. Twelve years after their wedding, the couple renewed their marriage vows in South Africa with Desmond Tutu officiating. Washington supports Nelson Mandela's children's fund and is a spokesperson for the Boys and Girls Club.

What threads of Washington's life and career weave back into a past life? Taking into consideration that he has played a military man in one of his first theater performances and at least five films, there's no doubt that Washington has been in the military in at least one past life. Additionally, he performed his own hand-to-hand combat in some roles, trained at Fort Irwin for a role, and has made a generous contribution to assist recovering vets and their families.

The kid who was chosen as "Police Chief of the Day" has, as an adult, been cast as a variety of police officers, detectives, forensic experts, and lawyers. Fortunately, Washington escaped a life of crime while his early neighborhood friends weren't so lucky. A cop in a past life? A lawyer? Probably.

Washington originally studied biology with the hope of becoming a doctor. His major acting break came as the result of playing the six-year role of Dr. Chandler in TV's *St. Elsewhere*. Medicine is another possible past-life profession.

Washington switched his major to political science before ultimately majoring in journalism. In his acting career, he has played a journalist twice, after "interning" for 120 days with real-life reporters. Interests and skills from the past? It's no coincidence that his soul led him to journalism this time around.

Washington's favorite roles are socially-conscious dramas. For example, he played Malcolm X off-Broadway and for film. His son is named in honor of Malcolm X. He portrayed an anti-apartheid activist in South Africa in *Cry Freedom*. In *Glory*, another of his favorite roles, Washington portrayed a former slave turned Union Civil War soldier. Surely, Washington, who is known for his anger-driven tirades, was a political activist in a past life.

With all the roles and awards under his belt, Washington has achieved his desire to get better at his craft. While working on the award-winning movie *Philadelphia* together, Tom Hanks said that working with Washington was like "going to film school."[1] Hanks complimented his skills by saying that he learned more about acting by watching him than from anyone else. Washington, who stumbled on acting as a YMCA staffer, clearly has been an actor before.

Finally, Washington's father was a preacher, and Washington too played the role of preacher in the *Preacher's Wife*. Washington, who is a devout Christian, has considered becoming a preacher in this life as well. "A part of me still says, 'Maybe, Denzel, you're supposed to preach. Maybe you're still compromising. I've had an opportunity to play great men and, through their words, to preach. I take what talent I've been given seriously, and I want to use it for good."[2] Every day, he reads the bible. He has donated $2.5 million towards building a church in Los Angeles. Perhaps his calling harkens back to another time when he was a minister of souls.

Whatever Washington's past lives may be, it's clear that they have led him to raise social awareness while being a part of an industry that can magically entertain, uplift, and inform its viewers.

Chapter 33

* * *

Jeff Daniels

If Jeff Daniels hadn't decided on a career as an actor, he might have run his father's lumber yard in the small town of Chelsea, Michigan. At Central Michigan University, he studied theatre and earned a degree in English. In the summer of 1976, Daniels performed in four plays at the Eastern Michigan University drama school's repertory program. Daniel's first break came when a guest director invited him to New York to perform for the Circle Repertory Company.

Since then, Daniels has starred in New York productions on and off Broadway. On Broadway, he's won a Drama Desk Award, an Obie Award for *Johnny Got His Gun*, and was nominated for a Tony Award as Best Actor for his role in *God of Carnage*.

Daniels married his high school sweetheart and the couple decided to stay in Michigan to raise their three children. Daniels says he's willing to commute because he loves Michigan and thinks living there keeps him sane and balanced through his career's ups and downs. He says, "he does fireworks, shovels snow and lives life there."[1]

In Chelsea, Daniels turned a bus garage into a regionally acclaimed playhouse using lumber from his dad's company. The theater he manages has produced more than ten of the plays Daniels has written. Daniels is also a musician and songwriter who has created at least five albums, the proceeds of which he donates to the playhouse.

As for his rise in film, Daniels got a small part in 1981's *Ragtime*. His breakthrough role was as Debra Winger's husband in the Oscar-winning *Terms of Endearment*. As the lead in Woody Allen's *Purple Rose of Cairo*, Daniels received the first of four Golden Globe nods.

Daniels has been a versatile actor, playing dramas, comedies, romances, and thrillers; good guys and bad; epic leaders and stupid idiots. Apparently not taking himself too seriously, his slapstick role in the comedy *Dumb & Dumber* in 1994 made him $750,000 and positioned him in the limelight. Twenty years later, he and sidekick, Jim Carrey, have done another re-make.

With a 180-degree turn, Daniels played the refined college professor turned revered Civil War Colonel Joshua Chamberlain in the two-part TV series *Gettysburg*. Ten years later, he reenacted Chamberlain again, this time for the epic historic movie *Gods and Generals*.

For Hallmark's *Redwood Curtain*, Daniels played a troubled Vietnam veteran. He played a senator in the American version of *State of Play*. For the A&E TV movie *The Crossing*, Daniels played George Washington. Other roles range from a self-absorbed academic to a gangster and an archaeologist.

In *Good Night and Good Luck*, the story of famed newsman Edward R. Murrow in the McCarthy era, Daniels plays the director of CBS news. Currently, Daniels won the Emmy for the role of news anchor on the HBO series *Newsroom.*

What past-life clues come to light here? First and foremost, Daniels is a Civil War buff. His role as Colonel Joshua Chamberlain, both for TV and film, was his all-time favorite. He even wrote the foreword to the award-winning book, *A Distant Thunder: Michigan in the Civil War,* authored by Richard Bak. It seems clear that Daniels fought in the Civil War, probably as a Northern officer. As for being a soldier, he even described a Broadway colleague, James Gandolfini, as "a guy you'd want in your foxhole."[2] Daniels could have been in a Michigan regiment; he is very attached to Michigan.

Was he Chamberlain? Some of Chamberlain's Gettysburg photos do bare a resemblance to Daniels. Chamberlain, who hailed from Maine, was a college professor of rhetoric with no military training. After the war, Chamberlain served as the governor of Maine for four terms. Interestingly, Daniels has a college degree in English, and he has portrayed an academic and a senator in films. It's possible that Daniels could have been Chamberlain.

It also is possible that Daniels was a reporter or writer in another lifetime. He has run newsrooms in both a film and an HBO series. Portraying a newsperson committed to national and international issues as well as portraying a senator and George Washington, it's also possible that he's been a politician in the past. With a degree in English, he has written more than a dozen plays for his playhouse. He could even have been a novelist.

In this lifetime, Daniels is also a songwriter. Daniels loves performing and enjoys guitar gigs. A musician, theater actor and playwright before? Seems likely. Because he has the ability to be so silly in front of the masses, he must have enjoyed making people laugh as a court jester or a roving troubadour as well.

But the down-to-earth award-winning actor, who exudes Midwest values and makes the viewer feel that he really does shovel snow and watch fireworks with his high school sweetheart and his family, has the ability to relate to everyman in his acting. He's at peace with himself and his roles, whether he's a goof or a general, in this life or the past.

Chapter 34

* * *

Taylor Swift

By the age of eleven, Taylor Swift dragged her mother to Nashville so that she could distribute demos to record companies in the hope of landing a record contract. Months later, a computer repairman showed her how to play three guitar chords. By twelve, she had taught herself to play guitar and was writing songs.

Today, Swift, who is the second best selling digital singles artist in the U.S. and earned over $64 million in 2014, still sees herself as a girl who writes songs in her bedroom. Swift is the youngest artist to be named Entertainer of the Year by the Country Music Association.

Growing up on a Christmas tree farm in Pennsylvania between the coal miners and the Amish, Swift was put in her first saddle when she was nine months old. Riding became her first hobby, and she later competed in horse shows.

Inspired by her grandmother, an opera singer, the child found herself, at nine, interested in musical theater. She made frequent trips to Broadway for singing and acting lessons and performed in plays such as *Grease, Annie,* and *The Sound of Music.* After a few years of not getting any acting roles in New York, her interest turned to country music. By ten, she was singing at fairs, coffee houses, and contests as well as singing the National Anthem at a Philadelphia 76ers game.

As a youngster, Swift loved to write poetry and tell stories. Even as a toddler, when she was singing to Disney movie soundtracks, she would often make up her own words. After her first round of record company refusals at age eleven, she began writing and playing her own music.

By the time she was in eighth grade, Swift had showcased her original songs in Nashville and was given an artist development deal by RCA Records. When she was fourteen, her family moved to Nashville to allow her to pursue her obsession with country music. Showcasing her talents again, she signed with an independent label and by sixteen released her debut album, which put herself on the map as a country music star. Swift was described as a "prodigy." A *Rolling Stone* critic compared the style of one melody to a combination of "Britney and Patsy."[1]

For her first single, "Tim McGraw," Swift and her mom stuffed CD's into envelopes and sent them to radio stations. She then followed up by sending baked cookies to radio programmers who played her song. A unique approach, to be sure. She also was one of the first country performers to use social media. Her third single, "Our Song," made her the youngest person to single-handedly write and perform a number one song on the *Hot Country Songs Chart.* The teen, wearing a sundress and cowboy boots, was recognized at the 2008 Grammy's when she was nominated for "Best New Artist."

Swift's second album, *Fearless,* a crossover to pop, became the best-selling album of 2009 in the U.S. winning four Grammys. Swift was the youngest singer to win "Album of the Year." The single "Mean" from her third album also won two Grammys.

Since then, Swift has straightened her hair and wears slinky outfits and red lipstick. She has changed her sound. She lives in a penthouse in New York. She pampers her core fan club, inviting them to her home.

She has also been the only singer to have three albums sell more than one million copies in a week. She is one of the world's best-selling artists of all time. Her awards include seven Grammys, twelve Billboard Music Awards, eleven Country Music Association Awards, and seven Academy of Country Music Awards.

Swift, the girl who has written songs on school notes, journals, and in sessions after high school, has been honored by the "Nashville Songwriters Association" and the "Songwriters Hall of Fame."

As an actress, Swift has appeared in small roles as a high school girl in the comedy *Valentine's Day,* an environmentalist in the animated film *The Lorax,* and the daughter of a chief in *The Giver.*

As a humanitarian, Swift supports music and arts education, children's literacy, natural disaster relief, anti-discrimination efforts, and aid for sick children.

As for a past life, it's obvious that a girl who liked country music even though it alienated her from her classmates, passed out her CDs to record companies at eleven, and broke her eighth grade contract with RCA records because she felt she was running out of time, was a country recording artist before, thus the rush and confidence to get out of the RCA contract while still in school. Swift has clearly been a singer and performer before.

As for the songwriting, besides being a songwriter in the past, perhaps she was a poet or writer in a prior life. Swift loves American history and the time periods around Ellis Island, the Founding Fathers, Abraham Lincoln and the Kennedys. Perhaps she was an early American who rode a horse in one or more of those time periods, even living during the time of President Kennedy since she gravitates to the '60s.

Chapter 35

* * *

Mat Franco

At the age of four, Mat Franco became obsessed with learning magic. Seeing magic performed first on television, Franco learned to videotape the shows and watch them repeatedly in slow motion until he could figure out the tricks. The self-taught Rhode Island boy's passion for the art of magic grew.

He demonstrated his craft on his first audience, his kindergarten class. His grandmother spent hours for years supporting him as he progressed. His parents drove him to birthday parties and church functions in church basements to work his magic.

As a twelve year old, his goal was to perform magic at the Radio City Music Hall. Using money he had earned from local shows, Franco traveled to Las Vegas to study magic and learn from some of the most famous magicians.

Later as a teen, Mat returned to Las Vegas and was paid to perform for other magicians at the Society of American Magicians National Convention. He also won several awards in state and national contests.

Franco, whose top priority has always been learning magic, says "he has dedicated his whole life to magic."[1]

With a marketing degree from the University of Rhode Island, Franco parlayed his understanding of college life and college students' humor into his new target audience. Franco's shocking interactive magic show became a favorite of campuses across the country.

In 2014, Franco auditioned for NBC's *America's Got Talent*. For the audition, he created a story by playing cards—all of which were selected by the judges. In the next episode, the cards created an image of judge Howie Mandel. In another competition, he dropped judge Mel B's phone into water, then while drying it off, the phone disappeared. It was found inside an audience member's seat cushion with the seat number of the three cards picked earlier by the judges.

Franco's best trick of all was becoming the first-ever magician to win *America's Got Talent*. Amazingly, the performance was at Radio City Music Hall. By 25, he had achieved his boyhood dream. A springboard to national and international attention, he won $1,000,000 and a headline show in Las Vegas.

Although his innovative tricks are hard to figure out, it's not difficult to discern that Franco was a magician and entertainer in several lifetimes. His obsession with magic at age four, his unending commitment, and the fact that he learned the craft all by himself indicates that he has performed as a magician professionally many times before. Houdini returned? Past life believers might say yes.

Chapter 36

* * *

Tommy Lee Jones

While many actors struggle and pay their dues, Tommy Lee Jones landed his first Broadway role ten days after graduating from Harvard and got an agent with a simple letter of introduction.

Jones, an eighth-generation Texan, was born in San Saba, Texas. He was the only child of a mother who was a police officer and beauty shop owner and a father who was a cowboy who worked in the oil fields. Like his father, for a while Jones worked on an oilrig; he also did underwater construction.

Because his father was so abusive, Jones worked to get a scholarship at an elite Dallas prep school so that he could stay in Texas while his father moved to North Africa for a job in the oil fields. He did, and then Jones got another scholarship to Harvard, where he played football and roomed with future Vice President Al Gore. As an English major, Jones loved drama and performed in school plays, gaining the lead in a Shakespeare production.

After graduating cum laude, Jones played roles on and off Broadway, had a supporting role in the film *Love Story*, written by a college friend, and spent four years as Dr. Mark Toland on the daytime soap opera *One Life to Live*.

After moving to Los Angeles, he appeared in more than 30 films and TV projects over the next twenty years. His 1977 role in the TV miniseries *The Amazing Howard Hughes* propelled him into the national limelight. His physical and vocal resemblance to Hughes was described as "uncanny." He then went on to earn an Emmy for his role as a murderer in *The Executioner's Song* and an Academy Award nomination for best supporting actor in Oliver Stone's *JFK* for his role as a suspected conspirator in the assassination. Other critically acclaimed roles include a Texas Ranger in the CBS miniseries *Lonesome Dove* and the husband of Loretta Lynn in *Coal Miner's Daughter*.

Two action thrillers made Jones an A-lister. The first was Jones' role as a rogue ex-CIA agent in *Under Siege*. Jones' breakthrough role in *The Fugitive*, as a U.S. marshal who relentlessly pursues a doctor wrongly convicted of killing his wife, won him an Oscar.

He's played a villain in *Batman Forever*, Agent K in the *Men in Black* series, a radical Republican congressman in *Lincoln*, and U.S. Army General Douglas MacArthur in the film *Emperor*.

As for his directing, Jones first attempt was *The Three Burials of Melquiades Estrada*, in which his character speaks both English and Spanish. It is a true story of the killing of an American teen in Texas by U.S. Marines. For TV, he also directed and co-wrote *The Good Old Boys* about an aging cowboy who must choose between freedom and family responsibility.

In his personal life, Jones is married to his third wife, longtime girlfriend, photographer Dawn Laurel. Jones lives in a suburb of San Antonio, is a part-time cattle rancher who owns two ranches including a 3,000 acre cattle ranch in San Saba County and another ranch near Van Horn, Texas, as well as a home and farm in the polo mecca of Wellington, Florida and a house in a polo country club in Buenos Aires, Argentina.

Jones is a champion polo player and raises polo ponies. His team won the U.S. Western Challenge Cup in 1993, and he invites top polo players from Harvard to practice at his ranch each fall. He supports the Polo Training Foundation. Such a specialized hobby, and Jones' intense commitment to it, is a past-life indicator. Polo has been played in Asia since the 6th century B.C. and was valued for its training for cavalry by the Middle Ages. British military officers imported the game to Britain in the 1850s. British settlers imported the game to the Argentine pampas. Some people believe that English Texans brought the game to the U.S. in 1876.[1]

It seems obvious that Jones was a polo player before, probably in Texas and in Argentina as a gaucho. He speaks Spanish fluently. Jones, who played several military officers including General MacArthur, also could have been a British officer and polo player in the 1850s as well as an American officer in World War II.

As for other obvious past-life clues, it's no doubt that Jones, an avid horseman, was a rancher in Texas in another lifetime. Besides the ranches he owns in Texas today, two films he directed, and one of which he co-wrote, involved ranchers in Texas. In several other roles he played a rancher as well, and many of his films are set in Texas. One of Jones' trademarks is his thick Texas accent.

In addition to his propensity to portray ranchers and Texans, Jones consistently plays hard-nosed law enforcement officers. He has played a Texas Ranger, a sheriff, and a marshal. Ironically, Jones' mother had been a police officer. It's extremely likely that Jones was a Texas Ranger, a sheriff, or a marshal before.

As for a past-life as an actor, Jones' lucky break, getting a role on Broadway less than two weeks after graduation and getting an agent after writing one letter, could have been a synchronistic experience. These seemingly random acts might really have been meant to be. Such events could be a clue to Jones' past life as an actor or performer.

The award-winning actor summed up his life interests, and some of his past life clues, when he said, "I love cinema and I love agriculture."[2] Sounds about right for Jones in this life, and likely in other lives as well.

Chapter 37

* * *

Ellen DeGeneres

Following Presidents George H. W. Bush and Bill Clinton to the podium to address the 2006 Tulane University graduates, comedienne Ellen DeGeneres came out dressed in a bathrobe and furry slippers. She said she was told that everyone would be wearing robes.

DeGeneres was born in a suburb of New Orleans to an insurance salesman and a speech therapist. Her parents were devout Christian Scientists. DeGeneres' mother described her daughter as a happy child with a happy childhood. When she was a teen, her parents divorced and the mother and daughter moved to Texas. DeGeneres used humor to cheer up her mother as well as fit in at new schools. As a youngster, DeGeneres dreamed of becoming a veterinarian but decided she wasn't book smart.

After high school, DeGeneres attended university for one semester but dropped out. She worked at J.C. Penney, sold vacuum cleaners, waited tables, and worked as a legal secretary.

DeGeneres started doing stand-up comedy at local clubs and coffee houses, eventually emceeing at Clyde's Comedy Club. She was known for her short, punchy jokes. When she won a Showtime cable TV competition as "The Funniest Person in America," she moved to San Francisco and gained national recognition doing her routine of "a telephone call to God" (inspired by a friend's tragic death) on *The Tonight Show.* Johnny Carson was impressed. The floodgates opened and DeGeneres became a regular on the talk show circuit.

In 1994, ABC created the TV sitcom *Ellen*, which showcased DeGeneres and her comic routines. It ran for four seasons and received two Emmy nods. When DeGeneres' character, and DeGeneres herself, announced that she was a lesbian, the show lost sponsors and was eventually cancelled.

After a few roles on the big screen, CBS launched *The Ellen Show* in 2001. In 2003, the pantsuit-wearing blond was back in full force with *The Ellen DeGeneres Show.* The show won 25 Emmys in the first three seasons. By mid-2009, she had hosted 1000 episodes, even hosting one from a hospital bed.

In addition to winning thirteen Emmys and fourteen People's Choice Awards, DeGeneres has hosted the Academy Awards, The Grammys, and the Primetime Emmys. While hosting the 2014 Academy Awards, DeGeneres took a selfie with Meryl Streep and other Oscar celebrities. The photo was retweeted 1.8 million times in the first hour, breaking the previous retweet record.

In her personal life, DeGeneres, also an author of three books, married long-time girlfriend Portia de Rossi in 2008. The vegan and meditator is a gay rights and animal rights activist.

Wanting to be a veterinarian as a youngster and being an animal rights activist and vegan, DeGeneres must have worked with animals in a past life, perhaps on a farm or in their natural habitat.

DeGeneres is a national, if not worldwide, spokesperson for gay rights. Some past-life regressionists speculate that we change sex in our various lifetimes. If that is a possibility, could it be possible that DeGeneres, who feels comfortable in suits and blue sneakers, was a male in her immediate past life? Could this be one reason why we are attracted to certain people or sexes and not others in our lives?

Finally, DeGeneres is in the funny business. She is a unique observer of people and human nature. She finds joy in making people laugh. Most probably, she has been a court jester or entertainer before. Because of her heightened powers of observation, she could have been a therapist or writer in the past as well.

Being genuine, DeGeneres seems to be living her truth. She paid a heavy price for her honesty with a temporary career setback. "Find out who you are and be that person. That's what your soul was put on this Earth to be," she says.[1] "I'm glad I'm funny and make people happy...but I'm proud to be known as a kind person."[2] That's a lot of wisdom coming from someone who could be swept away with her current stardom and salaries in excess of $15,000,000. With this kind of spiritual perspective, who, in the end, can ask for more?

Chapter 38

* * *

Daniel Day-Lewis

Because he was rejected for an apprenticeship as a cabi-netmaker, Daniel Day-Lewis decided to go into theatre.

Born into a wealthy London lifestyle, Day-Lewis was the son of England's Poet Laureate Cecil Day-Lewis and actress Jill Bacon. Her father was the head of Ealing Studios. When he was two, the family moved to South London. The tough South London kids often tyrannized Day-Lewis. In self-defense, he learned the local accent and demeanor and considers these confrontations to be his earliest acting classes. As a youth, he was often in trouble for petty crimes.

He didn't fare much better in public school. His parents sent him to board at a private school in Kent. Although he hated it, he discovered he liked to act, but was even more fascinated with woodworking and working class pursuits. Two years later, he was transferred to another independent school, Bedales in Hampshire. While there, at fourteen, he was paid two pounds to damage expensive cars for his first role as a hoodlum in *Sunday Bloody Sunday*.

After having worked the docks and done construction, he decided it was time for a career choice. Day-Lewis, who had been a good actor with the National Youth Theatre in London, applied to be trained as a cabinetmaker. Leaving it to destiny, he also applied for only one theatre school. He was denied training as a cabinetmaker but was accepted at the Bristol Old Vic Theatre School. He studied traditional acting for three years and was on stage at the British Old Vic and the Royal Shakespeare Company.

His first credited movie role was a small part in *Gandhi*. He continued to hone his craft with theatre performances and appearances on British TV. Intensely driven, Day-Lewis developed into a method actor who passionately absorbed his characters—in body, mind, and soul—and is known for his arduous research.

In 1984, he appeared on the silver screen as a conflicted first mate in *The Bounty*. His next two roles, as a gay man in an interracial relationship in the 1980s in *My Beautiful Laundrette* and as an upper crust fiancé in Edwardian England in *A Room with a View,* showcased his range of acting abilities. For both roles, the New York Film Critics named him Best Supporting Actor. For his first lead role in *The Unbearable Lightness of Being*, he learned Czech and stayed in character for eight months.

Day-Lewis won his first Academy Award for Best Actor for playing a paralyzed man in *My Left Foot*. He actually may have injured several ribs because he remained hunched over in a wheelchair and, to stay in character, had the crew wheel him around off-camera.[1] After a break from film, he returned to take the lead in *The Last of the Mohicans*. For the role, he always carried a rifle, even to a Christmas dinner. He learned to camp, hunt and skin animals, and build a canoe.

In preparation for portraying an Irishman falsely accused of being involved in an IRA bombing in *In the Name of the Father*, he spent time in a prison cell and had the cast verbally and physically mistreat him. For *The Boxer*, Day-Lewis trained with a world champion. He described boxing as requiring "resilience, heart, and self-belief even after its been knocked out of you."[2] The method actor has been dubbed "the English De Niro," because De Niro is also known to be fanatical about preparation and had trained as a boxer for a film.

After filming *The Boxer*, Day-Lewis took one of many hiatuses. He moved to Florence, Italy where he recharged by apprenticing himself as a cobbler. He was lured back to New York on a pretense but was recruited for his role as a brutal gang leader in *Gangs of New York*, for which he was nominated for another Academy Award. During shooting, he got sick because he refused to trade his tattered coat for a warmer one that wasn't authentic for that time period. He talked with a New York accent, even off set, and sharpened knives at lunch.

In 2004, Day-Lewis played a ruthless oilman in Southern California's oil boom of 1889 in the epic drama *There Will Be Blood*. He prepared for two years by reading correspondence of abandoned wives and men reduced to animalism because of their frantic scramble for "cheap money." For that performance, Day-Lewis earned another Oscar.

His most recent Academy Award was for his portrayal of Present Lincoln in Steven Spielberg's biopic *Lincoln*. For the role, Day-Lewis prepared for one year, reading over 100 books and working with a makeup artist. He says that for the role, he had the ability to create the illusion that part of him could believe without questioning (that he was Lincoln). "I never felt that depth of love for another human being that I had never met...I wish he had stayed with me forever."[3]

Often, Day-Lewis gets so involved with his characters that he has a hard time disengaging. He describes a "sense

of bereavement" because he doesn't want to leave the character behind. "You feel profound emptiness...It can take years
before you can put it to rest."[4]

What does help the actor disengage is plenty of down
time in his beloved, peaceful home in Ireland, his woodworking, and his family. Day-Lewis is married to Rebecca Miller,
the daughter of writer Arthur Miller. The couple met on the
set of Miller's *The Crucible.* Together, they have two children.
Day-Lewis has an older son from a previous relationship as
well. Even his wife and family aren't immune to the actor's
total immersion in his roles. Even though his wife was the
director of *The Ballad of Jack and Rose,* the actor lived alone
in a hut on Canada's Prince Edward Island beach during the
filming so that he could remain in character.

As for past-life clues, Day-Lewis spurned his well-to-do
life and education and identified with, even looked up to,
the working class. He applied to apprentice as a cabinetmaker and "makes his living" as a shoemaker. Even in theatre,
he admired the work of working-class writers. There's no
doubt that Day-Lewis has been in the working class before,
perhaps in many lives. He's probably been a cabinetmaker
in the British Isles, as well as a shoemaker, perhaps in Italy in
the Middle Ages.

Even though he's British, Day-Lewis also identifies with
Ireland. He loves what he describes as "a quality of wildness
that he relates to solitude."[5] Although some might think of
his move from England to Ireland as a betrayal, the country
seems to evoke a yearning of his soul.

Since his father was Irish, he visited yearly from the time
he was a child. From the first day he arrived, everything
seemed exotic. He claims that "his sense of Ireland's importance has never diminished...Just the sound of the west of
Ireland in a person's voice can affect me deeply."[6] Day-Lewis,
now holding dual citizenship, clearly lived in west Ireland
in the past. The landscapes and the accents are past-life

triggers that haunt him into retrieving parts of his past-life feelings.

Besides Ireland, Day-Lewis has had a secret love of American movies. He loves the infinite possibilities he sees in America, the opposite of the class system in Britain. As a youngster, he went to all-night screenings of Clint Eastwood's westerns and is said to love the concept of the untamed west. Coincidentally, Day-Lewis was cast in *The Last of the Mohicans* where he really became fascinated with the history of America. For the movie, he fully embraced the life, never being without his twelve-pound flintlock and rolled his own cigarettes.

For his role in *There Will Be Blood*, he was also back in the west, that time during the California oil rush in 1889. It is clear from his attraction to America's early west that Day-Lewis was there before. As for his role as a gang leader in 1862 lower Manhattan, New York, Day-Lewis could also have been an American immigrant.

Day-Lewis, who empathizes with the common man, also played American President Lincoln. Perhaps he was a politician around the time of Lincoln, fighting to protect the rights of the slaves.

Finally, the only three-time Academy Award winner for Best Actor, Day-Lewis has most certainly been an actor before. The genius, who was knighted for his service to drama, perhaps shied away from acting as a youth and preferred to experience real life first. Perhaps he remembered being cut off from real life as an actor in a past life and wanted to get to the depths of feeling so that, ultimately, he could be a better actor.

His deep, exhaustive preparations for his dramatic, emotional performances, as well as his long hiatuses, may allow him to tap into his own soul, the collective unconscious and his past-life experiences. Day-Lewis, "half-street urchin and half-good boy,"[7] was brought up in a privileged literary upbringing and works as a cobbler. He considers his loyalties to Ireland, America, and American movies as "heresies" and "dichotomies" and a disavowal of Britain, the hierarchical system and the traditional theatre system.[8]

Day-Lewis always knew that he could straddle two different worlds because he grew up in two different worlds. "If you can grow up in two different worlds, you can occupy four or six. Why put a limit on it?"[9] Day-Lewis is extremely selective about the roles he chooses. He believes that "you can never fully put your finger on the reason why you're suddenly, inexplicably compelled to explore one life as opposed to another."[10]

Maybe if he understood that perhaps he has lived many times before, in many countries, cultures, lifestyles and circumstances, he would understand the reason why he selects his roles. He would also realize that he had indeed been true to himself after all, could release his own sense of banishment, and integrate this awareness and his passions into a sense of wholeness.

Chapter 39

* * *

Cate Blanchett

Bored with her study of economics, Cate Blanchett left Australia and was vacationing in Egypt when she stumbled into a small role in an Egyptian boxing movie. Energized about acting and deciding this was an omen, Blanchett returned to Australia and threw herself into learning the craft at the National Institute of Dramatic Art (NIDA).

Blanchett was born in a suburb of Melbourne to a mother who was an Australian teacher and property developer and a father from Texas who worked in advertising. Her parents met when her father's naval ship was docked in Melbourne. Blanchett's father died when she was ten and her mother raised her and her two siblings with the help of their grandmother.

Describing herself as "part extrovert, part wallflower,"[1] Blanchett's first taste of acting came at Methodist Ladies'

College. From there, she went on to study economics at the University of Melbourne and then got a bit part in an Arabic boxing movie. It slaked her thirst and found her receiving acclaim from critics and the public alike, just a year after her graduation from the NIDA. Recognition from her stage performances led to TV roles, including ABC's *Heartland* drama, *Bordertown, G.P.,* and the *Police Rescue* series.

Her first role on the silver screen was as a nurse captured by the Japanese in World War II in the 1997 drama *Paradise Road.* By 1998, at 29, she had her breakthrough film role as Queen Elizabeth I in *Elizabeth,* for which she won a Golden Globe and Oscar nomination. Nine years later, she once again played Queen Elizabeth I in *Elizabeth: The Golden Age.* The film, which focuses on Elizabeth's later life, won her more nominations.

With versatility and grace, Blanchett transitioned from a royal monarch to a royal elf queen, Galadriel in the *Lord of the Rings* trilogy as well as *The Hobbit* trilogy. Blanchett has since bronzed her elf ears and claims she always wanted to wear pointy ears in a movie. In 2015, she portrayed a wannabe royal as the cold, cruel stepmother in *Cinderella.*

A six-time Oscar nominee, she received an Oscar nod for her role as Katharine Hepburn, girlfriend of Howard Hughes in *The Aviator,* and Best Actress Oscar for her lead as a rich New York socialite who becomes homeless in Woody Allen's *Blue Jasmine.* Other Oscar nominations include her role as an art teacher having an affair with her student in *Notes on a Scandal* and for her portrayal of legendary musician Bob Dylan in *I'm Not There.*

Blanchett's other notable films include an heiress in *The Talented Mr. Ripley,* an American wife wounded by a terrorist in Morocco in *Babel,* soviet agent in *Indiana Jones and The Kingdom of the Crystal Skull,* and the love interest of Brad Pitt who ages backwards in *The Curious Case of Benjamin Button.*

In *Charlotte Gray*, Blanchett portrays an English woman who became part of the French resistance movement in World War II. In *The Monuments Men*, with George Clooney, Blanchett, a French curator, helps the Allies recover art stolen by Nazis. Blanchett, has had a dream of performing in Berlin, but had dismissed it because she doesn't speak German. In *The Good German*, she played a Jew married to a German SS officer in Berlin just as World War II ends. Blanchett, the former lover of the American journalist played by George Clooney, is given a visa to the U.S. Could this be past-life recall through a dream or a premonition fulfilled?

With her outstanding abilities as a variety of characters with different accents, her Irish brogue was spot-on with her gripping portrayal of the Dublin reporter, *Veronica Guerin*, who was murdered for her investigation into the local drug trade in1996. In at least two movies, Blanchett was the love interest of a reporter.

The accomplished actress met her husband, writer Andrew Upton, in 1997 on a movie set. Both had an immediate aversion to each. He thought she was distant, while she thought he was haughty. They re-met at a party during a poker game. Three weeks later they were engaged and married quickly after that. The couple has three sons. The family lived in Brighton, England but moved back to Australia in 2006. They live in a Sydney suburb in a renovated 1877 sandstone mansion near the water. The couple served as artistic directors and co-CEOs of the Sydney Theatre Company from 2008 to 2013.

Politically, Blanchett is an advocate for women's rights, feminism and politics.

So, where does this award-winning journey lead as far as past-life clues? Although Blanchett asks herself whether she ever really wanted to be an actor, a synchronistic experience, getting a bit part in an Egyptian movie, nudged her into taking the plunge. Maybe it was meant to be.

Blanchett believes in timing, even in relation to meeting her husband. "I think we collided with each other at what turned out to be the perfect time," she says.[2] Either a strong immediate like or strong dislike at first sight can be indicative of a relationship in the past. It seems Blanchett and her husband Upton have known each other before. Also, it's no accident where they set up residence. If their mansion is any indication, maybe they lived in Sydney in the late 1800's. Blanchett also loved living in Brighton, England, describing it as "magical." It sounds like a happy past lifetime there.

The role that put Blanchett on the international map was as Queen Elizabeth I. She has played the role twice and has won dozens of awards. Blanchett even admits to liking to wear corsets. It is quite likely that she was in Queen Elizabeth's court and had some influence with the policies. In a time when the Queen was pressured to be married, Elizabeth ruled on her own devices. Today, Blanchett is an advocate of women's rights and politics.

Looking at Blanchett's strange fantasy to perform in Berlin, it is noteworthy that she portrayed a German Jew married to an SS officer in World War II. It is also interesting that she has portrayed a resistance fighter in France and a French curator in league with the Allies. In a fourth World War II film, Blanchett played an Australian nurse who was a Japanese prisoner of war. Surely, Blanchett was involved in World War II in her most recent past life, perhaps in league with the Allies.

Finally, her riveting portrayal of an Irish reporter, and her involvement with two other reporters in other films, as well as her potent political feelings, could make a strong case for her being a reporter or writer in another lifetime.

The Australian award-winning actress claims interest in "the gap between who we project to be and who we really are."[3] Perhaps the woman who grew up as "half wallflower" and seems very private, divulges more of her inner self than she realizes in the roles she selects. Whatever she projects at any given moment is so much richer than the economist or accountant she may have become were it not for synchronicity during a seemingly random vacation. Perhaps she has already had a quiet, private existence as an accountant in the past.

Chapter 40

* * *

Kate Winslet

It was only after Kate Winslet pounced on her father in the sand during a beach vacation that he consented to let the youngster attend drama school. Describing herself as wayward, passionate, and determined, she says," when I make up my mind to do something, there's no stopping me."[1] Winslet always wanted to act.

Winslet, who was born in Reading, England, grew up in a family of actors. Both her parents and an uncle were stage actors and her grandparents ran a repertory theatre. As a youngster, she got her first paycheck for dancing in a cereal commercial. At eleven, she studied the performing arts seriously at the Redroofs Theatre School. In addition to excelling, she was bullied and called "blubber" for her weight. After slimming down and graduating at fifteen, she appeared in theatre and the TV sitcom *Get Back*. There she met her first serious boyfriend, writer and actor Stephen Tredre, 28, and they lived together for nearly five years. He died of cancer shortly afterwards.

Reading the film script of *Heavenly Creatures* while in the back of her father's car, Winslet knew she had to get the role, that it was crucial to her life. With over 175 girls answering the casting call, the indomitable and confident seventeen year old won the role of an obsessive teen who helps to murder her best friend's mother. A novice, Winslet admitted to "not knowing a bloody thing" but directed her focus on becoming her character.[2] Her intense performance turned out to be her first big break, earning her critical acclaim.

At twenty, film star Emma Thompson singled her out of another casting call to accompany a star-studded cast in the period piece, *Sense and Sensibility* set in Kent in the 1790s. Winslet's plucky portrayal earned her a Supporting Actress Oscar nod, a mentorship and friendship with Thompson, and the role of Ophelia in Kenneth Branagh's *Hamlet* alongside another star-studded cast.

Once again, Winslet was determined to get the lead role as Leonardo DiCaprio's love interest, socialite Rose Bukater in *Titanic*. She lobbied the director, sending him a single rose with a card signed "From Your Rose." Her talent and persistence got her the role, which turned her into an international movie star and got her another Oscar nod for Best Actress, making her the youngest actress to get two nominations.

Escaping the instant stardom, Winslet returned home stating that, "she's an English girl who loves England."[3] She claimed that she'd rather do theatre and British films than move to Los Angeles in hopes of getting small roles.

After the blockbuster, the now-mega-star turned to some artsy, soul-searching roles such as a hippie on a spiritual quest in Morocco in the 1970s with her two daughters in *Hideous Kinky,* and the Australian devotee of a guru in *Holy Smoke.*

In *Quill*, Winslet was back in period dress as the maid and courier of the French Marquis de Sade. In France once again, she acted in the drama *A Little Chaos*, set in Versailles. In *Jude*, a Victorian period piece, Winslet portrayed a young suffragette.

Winslet continued to demonstrate her transformational versatility when, as a neurotic ex-girlfriend, she wore blue, orange, and pink hair in the science-fiction comedy drama *Eternal Sunshine of the Spotless Mind* with Jim Carrey.

Her roles have taken her into World War II at least twice: the first in *Enigma*, where she falls in love with a code breaker, and the second role in *The Reader* as a former Nazi concentration camp guard. Winslet, who received an Oscar for Best Actress, had a hard time sympathizing with her character.

Portraying a writer in *Iris*, Winslet plays the early life of Iris Murdoch. In the *Life of David Gale*, she is a reporter who interviews a death-row inmate.

As a young mother, Winslet lobbied for and got the role of mother of four in the blockbuster *Finding Neverland* with Johnny Depp. In another maternal role, Winslet portrayed a bored suburban housewife in *Little Children*. In the HBO miniseries *Mildred Pierce*, she plays a Depression-era mother who sacrifices for her self-absorbed daughter. In *Revolutionary Road*, she is a 1940s suburban housewife trapped by a pregnancy.

Winslet, who at the age of 33, was the youngest actress to receive six Oscar nominations and won an Oscar for Best Actress, has won an Emmy and a Grammy. Still, Winslet is determined to maintain balance in her life.

The mother of three has taken time off for her children, made their school lunches, and taken them to school. She is married for the third time. She thinks of herself as a British actress, not a movie star. Unlike her counterparts across the pond, she rides the tube while some of the Hollywood set are driven around in limos.

What past-life clues are exhibited by this British actress who became an overnight sensation? First, the fact that she was driven to be an actress and was intensively trained at the age of eleven is a past-life clue. The fact that she chose a family of actors could well indicate that they have all performed together in the past. Also, Thompson recognized her talents early in her career, which led to Winslet's ultimate selection for the role in *Titanic* and set her career on fire. Perhaps these directors recognized an innate talent that seems natural because it has been honed from other lifetimes. Both directors may have known and worked with Winslet before.

Known for her hourglass figure and period pieces, it's no doubt that Winslet has been a woman in Victorian England in the 1800s or Kent, England in the 1790s. She loves England and chooses to keep her home there. She's also probably lived in France, perhaps around the late 1600s. Winslet takes delight in being the rebellious Victorian women's libber. She probably was an advocate for changing the status quo in some of these lifetimes. In this life, she's an advocate for women not having to strive to be skinny, a new sign of beauty that was not popular in these prior periods.

That wayward willpower has given Winslet the confidence to make her own career and lifestyle choices and march to a different drummer. Even when she was thirteen and fourteen, she felt older than she really was. At fifteen, already out of school, having an acting career and living with her boyfriend, she was far more mature than most teens. In several previous lives, Winslet may have had to take on adult responsibilities at a young age.

Perhaps her rebellious choice of soul-searching roles after returning from Hollywood indicates that Winslet could have been into non-traditional religious beliefs in other lives. Maybe she was a British traveler to India or other cultures during the British colonial period and was exposed to other viewpoints and ways of life.

Like the roles she has selected to play, Winslet has most likely been in World War II before. Chances are that she was British since she had no empathy for the SS officer-character she portrayed, even though it garnered her the Oscar. Also, because of her two journalist roles, it's possible that she was a journalist or writer.

Winslet, who prioritizes her family above career, has played several maternal roles as well. Of course she has been a mother before. Perhaps in a recent life, even while performing, she put more emphasis on career and now is unwavering in putting her family first.

The award-winning Winslet is to be admired for her grace, presence, and artistic accomplishments as well for her balanced lifestyle, which prioritizes her family and includes a healthy perspective on fame.

Chapter 41

* * *

Jennifer Lawrence

While in New York on spring break with her parents, an agent discovered fourteen-year-old Jennifer Lawrence and set up a screen test. Her cold read was so impressive that the agent urged her to stay in New York for the summer. She did. The rest is history.

Born in Louisville, Kentucky, Lawrence's mother ran a summer day camp, and her father was a construction worker. While in school, she played softball, field hockey, was a cheerleader, and modeled. Lawrence graduated from high school with a 3.9 GPA two years earlier than her class so she could work on her acting. In New York, she acted in commercials and small roles.

After her family moved to Hollywood, Lawrence landed the role of a teenage daughter in the TV sitcom *The Bill Engvall Show*. Then, in *The Burning Plain*, she played a teen who left her baby in Mexico. For her role, she was recognized as best emerging young actress. Her first lead role, in *The Poker House*, was as a teen raising her two sisters in their mother's whorehouse.

Lawrence's breakthrough role came in *Winter's Bone* when she played a teen in the rural Ozarks who tracks her paroled father to stop her family's eviction. She says she would have "walked on coals for the part."[1] This garnered her Oscar and Golden Globe nods. At the time, at twenty, she was the second youngest person to receive an Academy Award nomination for Best Actress.

By 23, Lawrence won her Oscar for Best Actress for her role as a neurotic widow who helps a bipolar man train for a dance contest in the romantic comedy *Silver Linings Playbook*. She also plays an unstable wife in *American Hustle*. In *House at the End of the Street*, Lawrence is the daughter of a divorcee who befriends a boy whose family was massacred.

Despite her emotionally heavy portrayals, Lawrence doesn't allow herself to get drained by these roles. She doesn't invest her own emotions and doesn't take any of the characters' pain home at the end of a workday.

Moving to a lighter role in the superhero film *X-Men: First Class* and its sequel, Lawrence got the role of Raven/ Mystique, a shape-shifting mutant and childhood friend. She had to go on a diet, work out for two hours a day and got blisters from her elaborate body makeup.

The role of a lifetime, Lawrence was then cast as Katniss, the lead action heroine in *The Hunger Games* series. For the role, she was trained in stunts, archery, combat, military obstacle courses, and climbing. Now a solid A-lister, *The Hunger Games* series has made Lawrence the highest-grossing action heroine of all time. The films have even kicked off a new trend for young mothers who name their baby girls "Katniss."

Donald Sutherland, a cast member, describes Lawrence as an "exquisite and brilliant actor."[2] He compared her to

Lawrence Olivier. The film's director says that she makes her performance look easy and calls her acting "effortless."[3] Lawrence never took classes or had any experience in acting. She says that watching, listening, and studying people is the best acting class.

So, what about past-life clues for the fourteen year old who was discovered? The fact that she was discovered, after getting her parents to go to from Kentucky to New York to get an agent, is indicative of a belief that she was destined to act in this life, probably based on subconscious memories of having acted before.

Without ever having studied acting or been on a stage, her cold-reading and acting abilities, even as reported by seasoned actors and directors, is another past-life clue. Her talents point to her development of those skills through performing in other lifetimes.

Lawrence has clearly had at least one past life in New York, possibly as an actress or dancer. She says that when her feet first hit the sidewalks of New York, she felt as if she had been born and raised there. It's as if "she took over the town" and knew that she'd move there.[4]

A recurring theme in her roles is the maternal instinct. In *Winter Bone, The Hunger Games,* and *The Poker House,* Lawrence's characters care for younger siblings in dark situations. Even the job she describes before acting was as assistant nurse to children at her parents' camp. It seems that Lawrence may have had some poor lifestyles and painful relationships in past lives and has assisted her siblings before, but in her acting roles, she doesn't emotionally identify.

As for being a Maid Marian-type in medieval times with her bow and arrow, it is possible. At her California home, she was actually ready to let an arrow fly on a would-be thief in what turned out to be a false alarm.

An award-winning actress, Lawrence has already achieved more success and international fame than most actors and actresses aspire to. But it is clear that Lawrence, in the promising process of becoming, is on a trajectory that's upward-bound. There will be much more to uncover as self-discovery unfolds through portrayals of new challenging characters and perhaps even taking on the role of director.

Chapter 42

***

Keira Knightley

At the age of three, Keira Knightley asked her parents for an agent. By the age of six, she thought that she should be earning her own living. By seven, she had a role in a TV movie. As a youngster, she was totally focused on acting, mesmerized by the cinema, and trained in dance. Playing with dollhouses and making up stories inspired her to become an actress, mainly so that she could keep on playing make-believe.

Knightley, born in a London suburb, is the daughter of actor Will Knightley and actress and playwright Sharman Macdonald. Even though she didn't know what an agent did, she figured she should have one since her parents each had an agent. When it was discovered that she had dyslexic tendencies and couldn't read, her parents made a deal that if she would have a book in hand and a smile on her face throughout the summer vacation of her sixth year, she would get an agent.

By the end of the holiday, she had gotten her agent and, shortly after, a TV role in *Screen One: Royal Celebration*. As a youngster, she did amateur productions, commercials, and small TV roles.

Knightley appeared in several television films and, as a teenager with no formal training, got a major film break in the role of the Queen's look-alike decoy in *Star Wars Episode I: The Phantom Menace*. Juggling school, she played Rose in the TV miniseries *Oliver Twist*. Knightley's plucky role as friend of an Indian girl who wants to play soccer in *Bend It Like Beckham* is what brought her public recognition.

Knightly was propelled into international stardom through her role as Elizabeth Swann in the *Pirates of the Carribbean* movie series. Swann grows into a courageous pirate with inspirational leadership and seaman-like battle strategy skills. She protects herself with swords, knives, and firearms.

Since the *Pirates of the Caribbean* films, Knightley has done a range of period dramas. She's portrayed Laura in the TV miniseries *Doctor Zhivago*, set prior to the Russian Revolution and through the Civil War in the early 1900s. Ten years later, she starred as Anna Karenina, a wealthy socialite in 1874 Imperial Russia, in the film by the same name.

For her moving portrayal of the unmarried daughter Elizabeth in *Pride and Prejudice*, which takes place on a farm in rural England in the late 18th century, Knightley earned a Golden Globe and Oscar nomination. She loved Austen's book since she was seven and with her first check from acting, bought herself a doll's house of the central character, Mr. Darcy's mansion.

Then, as the 18th century Duchess of Devonshire, Knightley displays her beauty, fashion extravaganza, and gambling addictions in *The Duchess*. In the movie *King Arthur*, Knightley plays

Guinevere while Arthur is reinterpreted as a Roman officer in 467 A.D.

In the Oscar-winning movie *Atonement*, a British romantic war drama set from 1930 to 1990, Knightley, who portrays the lover of a man falsely accused of rape, was nominated for an Oscar for her poignant role. Knightley's character later became a nurse in World War II while her lover died in the war. Coincidentally, the following year, she plays a nightclub singer who marries a British World War II captain who suffers post-traumatic stress in *The Edge of Love*. In the 2014 *Imitation Game*, Knightley plays a code breaker during World War II.

In *The Jacket*, Knightley is a waitress/nurse who befriends a Gulf War vet suffering from amnesia and time travels. In *Jack Ryan: Shadow Recruit*, Knightley plays a medical student who helps a U.S. Marine, who was wounded in Afghanistan, learn to walk again.

In addition to her propensity to take on roles set during war times, Knightly also tends to perform in films set in Europe. In *A Dangerous Method*, which takes place just prior to World War I in Switzerland, Knightley plays a patient of Carl Jung who goes on to become one of the first female psychoanalysts. In *Silk*, Knightley is married to a 19th century French officer who becomes a silkworm trader. And, in 2015, Knightley makes her Broadway debut in *Therese Raquin*, set in the late 1800s in France, as an orphan and later a wife.

In her private life, Knightley is married to English musician James Righton of the Klaxons. Basically shy, she prefers quiet evenings at home with their family and friends. She supports human rights, promotes reading, and fights domestic violence.[1]

So, what can looking at Knightley's life and career tell us about her potential past lives? First, she's been an actress before. Growing up in an acting family, she wanted an agent at three and had her first role at seven. Our earliest memories and desires are an indication of what we have done before as a profession. In a case of synchronicity, Knightley nearly missed auditions for her first *Pirates of the Caribbean* role due to traffic. That put her at the end of the auditions. She attributes that to getting the job, ultimately making her an internationally-recognized name.

Knightley also has played in war movies, or with war-affected characters, at least six times. In four of them, she is in World War II. In three movies she plays a nurse or medical student. In one, she is a code breaker. It is very likely that Knightley has been in World War II before, perhaps as a nurse or the caretaker of a wounded warrior returned home.

Knightley, who loves England, has played an 18th century duchess and a gentrified woman in the late 18th century. She treasured the book *Pride and Prejudice* and purchased a doll's house of the mansion. She says, "the beauty of Elizabeth is that every woman...seems to recognize herself, with all her faults."[2] She received critical acclaim for her role in the movie adaptation of the book. It's very likely she was in England in the 19th century, probably as landed gentry.

With two roles under her belt set in Russia, it's also likely that she has been in Russia before, in the late 1800s or early 1900s. As for France, she's been in at least two movies and a play there as well. She was also married in Marseilles. These clues offer another geographical past-life connection through roles she has chosen or directors who have seen her as a match.

The shy performer, who sits in cafes and observes people, was the second highest paid actress in 2007. Even though, when she dresses for Awards ceremonies, she feels she's a five year old in her mother's clothes, she has achieved her six-year-old goal of earning her own living and has been able to continue playing and using her imagination and aptitudes as an actress.

Chapter 43

* * *

LeAnn Rimes

While sitting in her highchair, American singer LeAnn Rimes stunned her family by singing "Jesus Loves Me." Her parents remember being shocked with her enunciation and ability to remember the words. Before she could say a complete sentence or take her first step, she could sing.

The country and pop singer was born in Jackson, Mississippi and raised in Dallas, Texas, by high school sweethearts Belinda and Wilbur, who had a talent for singing with a perfect pitch. By two, Rimes had learned to tap dance, and at five, while taking dancing and singing lessons, she affirmed that she would be a big star. She performed at talent contests, rodeos, and sang "The Star Spangled Banner" to packed stadiums for Dallas Cowboys football games. Her father would order music tapes and Rimes would spend school nights and weekends rehearsing them.

By nine, she had a talent agent. By eleven, Rimes had recorded her first album on an independent label. It featured her song "Blue," which was originally written for singer Patsy Cline but shelved when she was killed in a plane crash. The songwriter, Bill Mack, said that it was a "hair-raising experience" when he heard Rimes sing the song because she sounded so much like Cline.[1] The media said her singing sounded like a young Patsy Cline and dubbed Rimes "The Next Patsy Cline."[2]

By thirteen, Rimes was a star. By fourteen, she had signed on with Curb Records. Curb's owner was stunned both that her rich vocals sounded so similar to Cline's and that she had a command of the history of music as well as an ear for pitch.[3]

By fourteen, she was the second youngest artist to be nominated for the Country Music Awards. "Blue" earned her a Grammy for Best Country Vocal Performance and one for Best New Artist, a feat never achieved by a country music artist. The fourteen-year-old star didn't think of herself as an overnight success. She said, "I've been at this since six."[4] It's the next step in the journey she's been on since she was a baby.

She began to cross over to adult contemporary and pop with *Unchained Melody: The Early Years* and *You Light Up My Life: Inspirational Songs*, which appeared on Pop, Country and Contemporary Christian *Billboard* charts at the same time. No other country singer had ever achieved this. Her single "How Do I Live" set a record for staying at the top of the *Billboard* chart for 69 weeks.

Patsy Cline was Rimes' major role model. In the album, *LeAnn Rimes*, she mainly selected songs, like "Crazy" and "I Fall to Pieces" by Cline.

A crossover pop hit, Rimes won a Blockbuster Entertainment Award for her song "Can't Fight the Moonlight" from the soundtrack of *Coyote Ugly*, the film in which she made her acting debut. Rimes also starred in a TV movie *Holiday in Your Heart,* which Rimes co-authored. The movie was based on her book.

In 2005, Rimes returned to country with *This Woman,* her best-selling album in five years. This garnered her nominations for a Grammy and an American Music Award. By 2007, Rimes was enjoying creative control and writing her own songs and released her album *Family.* It is likely, that she was a writer in a past life.

Rimes has sold 37 million records worldwide and has written two novels and two children's books. Her many achievements also include two Grammys, twelve *Billboard* Music Awards, and an American Music award. Rimes is married for a second time to actor Eddie Cibrian, who she met while filming the Lifetime TV film *Northern Lights.* She is an advocate for cancer research and gay rights.

For the little girl with the big job, who at times has 65 people on her payroll, what does her life say about a possible past life? There's no doubt that the baby in the highchair remembered singing in her immediate past life. The fact that Rimes' amazingly mature soprano voice and vocal style reminded music critics and record label owners of Patsy Cline is alluring. Even more remarkable is their labeling of Rimes as the successor to Cline's legacy. They compared her distinctive emotional expression in her first single "Blue" with that of Cline's style. Uncharacteristic of a youngster, Rimes was also known for choosing mature adult material.

An extraordinary synchronicity, Rimes' first hit, "Blue," was originally written for Cline but was mothballed after she died suddenly. Also interesting, is the fact that Rimes' father threw out the song, thinking it was not a match for his daughter. Rimes salvaged it from the wastebasket. It's also important that the songwriter had a "hair-raising experience" when he first heard Rimes sing "Blue."

It's a foregone conclusion that Rimes was a major singer in her last past life. It's quite possible that she indeed was her own role model, Patsy Cline. Rimes was convinced that she'd be a star and had the confidence and talent to follow through. She may have picked right up where she left off. Maybe she even knew the same significant people before, people like songwriter Bill Mack and Curb's record label owner.

Part of the early '60s country sound, Cline successfully crossed over to pop music, just like Rimes did. At eight, Cline taught herself to play piano. By sixteen, she performed on local radio stations. Similarly, Rimes learned to perform at a young age and had an agent by the time she was eleven years old. Cline felt stifled with her first record deal and signed with Decca three years later. Rimes wanted to break her record deal but renegotiated new terms that gave her more creative control. Both have won many awards and achieved mega-success in their teens and 20s. Cline died in a plane crash in 1963 when she was thirty. Rimes was born nineteen years later. Perhaps a few of those who called the fourteen year old "a young Patsy Cline" wondered whether she was, indeed, a young Patsy Cline.

As a teen, Rimes hit the ground running in Nashville and doors flew open for her. More comfortable in Nashville than Hollywood, Rimes' country fans love her. She is definitely here for a reason: to fulfill her destiny as a singer.

Chapter 44

* * *

Liam Neeson

Eleven-year-old Liam Neeson took the lead in his school play because the girl he was attracted to was slated as the leading lady. From then on, he continued to act in school plays. Neeson was also inspired to become an actor by watching the local Bible-thumping Presbyterian minister Ian Paisley. Neeson, who was raised Catholic, would sneak into the church to admire his presence, great acting, and stirring presentations.

Born in Ballymena, Northern Ireland to a cook and a school caretaker, Neeson was an amateur boxer, earning a broken nose and staying until he experienced black outs. He also was a forklift operator for Guinness and planned to become a teacher but quit college to join Belfast's Lyric Theatre and then moved to Dublin's Abbey Theatre. While performing classics, he was discovered and cast in his first high-profile film role as Gawain in *Excalibur.*

Neeson met actress Helen Mirren on set, and he moved to London and lived with her. Mirren helped him get an agent. In London, he found supporting roles in *The Bounty* and *The Mission.* When he moved to Hollywood, he got good reviews as a mute homeless man in *Suspect* and as lead man in the superhero action movie *Darkman.*

His role in the Broadway play *Anna Christie* gained him a Tony nomination, a future wife—his co-star, Natasha Richardson, and his breakthrough movie role as Oskar Schindler in Steven Spielberg's *Schindler's List.* For his starring role in the Academy Award-winning Holocaust film, he earned the Oscar, British Academy of Film and Television, and Golden Globe award nominations for Best Actor.

In high demand, Neeson then starred in three period pieces: as the 18th century Scottish Highlander *Rob Roy,* the Irish Revolutionary leader *Michael Collins,* and the ex-con-turned-industrialist Jean Valjean in *Les Miserables,* set in the French Revolution. Later, in another role set in 1184 France, Neeson plays a Crusader to the Holy Land in *Kingdom of Heaven.* In another Scottish role, in *The Big Man,* Neeson is a miner who loses his job during a union strike. In the film, in order to make money for his family, the miner agrees to box.

Because of Neeson's presence, strength, and amazing acting skills, director George Lucas selected Neeson as the Jedi Master Qui-Gon Jinn in *Star Wars: Episode I.* By *Star Wars Episode II,* only his incorporeal voice was heard. He also voiced Aslan, the wise lion and true king in *The Chronicles of Narnia* series. As king, he guides the children through their adventures. Neeson's voice is also used on a *Simpson's* episode; he performs as the voice of a Catholic priest who converts Bart and Homer.

In another fantasy adventure, *Clash of the Titans,* Neeson plays Greek god Zeus and orders Poseidon to unleash the last of the Titans. In *Batman Begins* and the *Dark Knight Trilogy*, Neeson unleashes his own "inner villain." The scriptwriter said the role was complex. "He's not bent on revenge; he's actually trying to heal the world. He's just doing it by draconian means."[1]

Back in the drama department, Neeson won a Tony for being the protagonist and an adulterer during the Salem witch trials in the Broadway production of *The Crucible*. In *Chloe*, Neeson also portrayed an unfaithful husband.

Neeson portrayed the head of an Irish Catholic gang who was killed early-on in *Gangs of New York*. In the TV drama *Five Minutes of Heaven*, Neeson plays a Northern Ireland loyalist convicted of killing a Catholic boy and reconciling with the family when he gets out of prison. In *Breakfast on Pluto*, Neeson is a Catholic priest in Northern Ireland in the late 1940s who has fathered a transgender orphan. In *Mission*, he is one of the Spanish Jesuits who builds a mission in the South American jungle in the 1750s.

As for military roles, Neeson plays a high-ranking Nazi officer whose nanny is an American spy in *Shining Through*. Neeson portrays a Russian officer in *K19: The Widowmaker* aboard the Soviet's deadly 1961 first ballistic missile nuclear submarine. In *The Bounty*, Neeson is a British naval corporal in the Pacific Ocean in 1787. At the end of the American Civil War, Neeson is a former Confederate officer turned bounty hunter in *Seraphim Falls*.

In the movie *The A-Team*, he is a former U.S. Army Special Forces officer falsely convicted of a war crime in Vietnam who works as a soldier of fortune to fight injustice. As a retired CIA operative in *Taken I*, he finds his kidnapped daughter. In *Taken II*, his daughter has to save he and his wife. After his wife is murdered in *Taken III*, he again fights to insure the safety of his daughter. In *A Walk Among the Tombstones*, he is a former police officer hired to track the killers of a drug dealer's wife.

Additional roles include *Kinsey*, a pioneer in "sexology" in 1948; a writer, father, and new widower in the feel-good film *Love Actually;* and a wolf-killer protecting an Alaskan oil drilling team in *The Grey*. In *Nell*, he is a small town doctor in North Carolina who finds a "wild child;" in *Unknown*, he's a doctor of biotechnology, who loses his memory and identity, and fouls an assassination attempt while at a conference in Germany.

In Neeson's personal life, he accomplished his goal: to win the leading lady. He met and married his co-star, Natasha Richardson, in the Broadway play *Anna Christie*. Together, they have two boys. Sadly, Richardson died of injuries resulting from a ski accident in Montreal in 2009.

What does the Irish actor's career and life tell us about possible past lives? One of the themes running through some of his more recent roles is as a mentor or father of a student or son who must struggle on, after Neeson's character dies early in the movie. Such films include *Batman Begins, Kingdom of Heaven, Gangs of New York* and *Star Wars I*. It is interesting that early on, Neeson planned on being a teacher. He has clearly been a teacher and role model in at least one lifetime.

Some of his mentoring roles also involve spiritual overtones and wisdom: like the Jedi Master in *Star Wars* and Aslan in *The Chronicles of Narnia*. Neeson said, "Aslan symbolizes a Christ-like figure, but he also symbolizes, for me, Mohammed, Buddha and all the great spiritual leaders and prophets over the centuries."[2] While filming in Istanbul, Neeson found the Islamic call to prayer a moving experience. He also appreciates St. Ignatius Loyola's Spiritual Exercises.

In his roles, he has played a priest at least twice, even converting Bart Simpson, as well as an Irish Protestant who kills a Catholic youth. He also played a Crusader who ultimately gives his life for the Catholic Church. Neeson was raised Catholic but reveled in the local Presbyterian minister Ian

Paisley's sermons. With his interest in the spiritual aspects of several religions, it would come as no surprise that Neeson had been a priest in one or more lifetimes and has also been involved in other religions and cultures in past lives.

Neeson has portrayed a military officer at least four times, not to mention CIA Special Ops and a police officer. He's been a Russian, British, American Confederate and Nazi officer. Perhaps his most prominent role as Schindler, a German company owner who has a list that keeps Jews alive, points to the distinct possibility that Neeson was a Freedom Fighter during the Holocaust. It's clear that he has also taken on military responsibilities, even clandestine activities, in other lives.

With his Irish heritage, and his roles as an Irish revolutionary leader, the 18th century Scottish leader *Rob Roy*, and a Scottish miner-turned boxer, not to mention Sir Gawain, knight of Arthur's Roundtable in *Excalibur*, Neeson has been in the British Isles before—perhaps as far back as the 15th century. Being an amateur boxer as a teen, Neeson was probably a boxer before.

Who could have imagined that out of Neeson's fantasy roles may have emerged a pattern of strength, mentorship, and spiritual wisdom that point to past lives as teacher and spiritual guide? In dramatic roles such as in *Schindler's List* and *Les Miserables*, the compassion of this tall, slender Irishman shines through. Surely this trait has been present in other lifetimes. Neeson is blessed to have had fifteen years with his leading lady and, as a "Master Actor" as identified by director George Lucas, has a worldwide creative outlet for his acting skills and screen presence.

Chapter 45

* * *

Benedict Cumberbatch

Born into a family line of prominent personages in British high society and with two actor-parents, Benedict Cumberbatch was sent to posh boarding schools from the time he was eight. At Harrow, one of the oldest, most prestigious schools in England, Cumberbatch studied art, painted large oil canvases, played rugby, and began to act.

Cumberbatch was born and raised in London to actors Wanda Ventham and Timothy Carlton. His grandfather, a submarine commander honored in World Wars I and II, was a member of the upper class; his great-grandfather was a diplomat.

Cumberbatch joined the drama club at Harrow, and at twelve, his first stage role was as the Queen of the Fairies in Shakespeare's *A Midsummer Night's Dream.* His drama teacher identified him as "the best schoolboy actor" he'd ever had.[1]

After Harrow, Cumberbatch took a year off to teach English in a Tibetan monastery. When he returned, he joined the drama department at Manchester University. He got an M.A. in Classical Acting from the London Academy of Music and Dramatic Art and procured an agent.

Once on the London stage, Cumberbatch received recognition for several roles. In *Hedda Gabler*, he plays a Norwegian husband who's interested in research and travel. In *After the Dance*, he's a 1920s aristocratic husband who trivializes life until his wife commits suicide. As Rosencrantz from *Hamlet*, he's a Danish noble who visits England in 1592. For his performance in the starring role in *Frankenstein*, he was awarded London Theatre's Triple Crown: the Olivier Award, Evening Standard Award, and Critics' Circle Theatre Award.

After several small roles on BBC television, Cumberbatch got the role as British scientist Stephen Hawking for a BBC TV movie. His performance got him his first co-lead movie role in *Amazing Grace* as William Pitt, the 18th century British prime minister who campaigned against slavery. Ironically, years later, Cumberbatch plays a Southern slave owner in *12 Years a Slave*.

Other BBC TV roles include a young aristocrat passenger on a British warship to Australia in the early 19th century, who deals with issues of class privilege and proper conduct, in the miniseries *To the Ends of the Earth*. In the play for TV, *The Turning Point*, he's a Soviet spy who works for the BBC. In *Small Island*, he's a London banker who suffers from post-traumatic stress from World War II. In the much-acclaimed BBC World War I miniseries *Parade's End*, which has been alluded to as "the highbrow Downton Abbey," Cumberbatch finds himself in a love triangle and also in uniform fighting in France. In another miniseries, *Dunkirk*, he is once again fighting in France as a British officer.

Cumberbatch's breakout role in the BBC series *Sherlock* Holmes, and its resulting coverage on PBS in the U.S., has assured Cumberbatch as an "A-lister" with international acclaim and an Emmy for Outstanding Lead Actor in a Miniseries.

On the big screen, his first appearance was in *To Kill A King*, which takes place at the end of the English Civil War. *Atonement* is set around World War II in Britain and in Dunkirk, France. In *The Other Boleyn Girl*, Cumberbatch is William Carey, husband of Mary Boleyn. In *Tinker Tailor Soldier Spy*, he is a British investigator involved in the hunt for a Russian double agent in the 1970s. And, in *War Horse*, he portrays a British major leading a cavalry unit in France in World War I.

In addition to *Amazing Grace*, Cumberbatch had a starring role in *Star Trek Into Darkness* as Khan, a genetically engineered superhuman, and in *The Fifth Estate*, as the Australian computer-hacker of the news-leaking website Wikileaks.

His most recent lead role in *The Imitation Game* as Alan Turing, the Nazi code breaker who creates the forerunner of the computer, has brought him critical acclaim and more international recognition. For his acting, he earned an Academy Award nomination for Best Actor, two Golden Globes and five Screen Actors Guild Award nominations. He has been selected as one of *Time* magazine's 2014 "Most Influential People in the World."

So, how does his life and career point to his past lives? The fact that Cumberbatch chose to travel to a Tibetan monastery to teach English indicates that he had a lifetime either as a Tibetan or as a foreigner who visited there. Finding meditation and mindfulness helpful, he subscribes to aspects of Buddhism. Because he decided to spend his free time in Northern India and was attracted to a religion and culture he did not grow up in, he probably gravitated to it because he was a Buddhist before.

While a student, he studied art and painted with oils. Such talents and interests at an early age reveal that he may have been an artist before.

Cumberbatch has been cast and re-cast as a British officer. His roles have been set in the English Civil War, World War I at least twice, and World War II at least three times fighting in France. In *Imitation Game*, Cumberbatch is a computer genius and Nazi code breaker. It's obvious the he has been a British officer, most recently in World War I and II.

Cumberbatch comes from an aristocratic family, some of whom have been distinguished in public service. He went to a famous boarding school. In many of his roles, he plays a British aristocrat or Danish noble. He experienced court life in the time of Henry VIII as husband of Henry's one-time lover Mary Boleyn. He also portrayed British Prime Minister William Penn, an advocate of abolishing slavery.

In this life, Cumberbatch originally thought about becoming a lawyer. As for social activism, he has protested the Iraq War, spending cuts for the arts, civil liberty violations in the British government, and is an advocate of gay rights. He plays homosexual Alan Turing in *The Imitation Game*. Surely, Cumberbatch has been an aristocrat and British politician in a past life.

Aside from playing upper-class roles, Cumberbatch plays men who are highly intelligent. He enjoys playing Sherlock Holmes and finds it challenging to be involved in a role that involves such a high level of intelligence and wit. He describes it as a "form of mental and physical gymnastics."[2] Other highly intelligent roles include portraying scientist Stephen Hawking, Alan Turing who was in the forefront of creating the computer, and the Australian computer hacker who founded Wikileaks. Perhaps Cumberbatch was an inventor, scientist, philosopher, or college professor in one or more lifetimes.

The British actor has lived his passion: acting. He knows that no matter what the preparation, "you are always yourself, always inside your own skin...an essential element of you...is what is in the present."[3] In this life, he feels as if he has lived "5,000 times over...I've seen and swam and climbed and lived and driven and filmed."[4]

And now, he's loved. Cumberbatch is married to theatre director Sophie Hunter and has a new role on the way, fatherhood, as well as a new villa in Tuscany. The couple were married on Valentine's Day, 2015 at a 12th century church, St. Peter and Paul on the Isle of Wight. The reception was held nearby, at the Mottistone Manor, a historic site once owned by Hunter's family.[5] The location could reveal another past-life site for Cumberbatch and his new family.

Cumberbatch has certainly carried into this life the talents of his soul. He is in touch with his acting skills from other times, his past relationships, his multidimensional selves, and his past lives on a subliminal level.

Chapter 46

* * *

Jay Leno

Comedic host of *The Tonight Show* for over two decades, Jay Leno has had an obsession with cars since he was a youngster. He bought a thirty-year-old Ford V-8 truck that didn't run when he was fourteen. Leno learned how to restore it before he got his license.[1] Four days after he got his license, he got in his first car accident.

Leno found a job at a Rolls-Royce and Bentley dealership. He claims that the thought of owning a Bentley inspired him to become an entertainer. He figured that acting was his only chance of ever owning a Bentley. He now owns several vintage Bentleys from the 1920s and '30s.

Leno was funny, even as a kid. He got his first laughs at four, when he innocently asked how come girls have humps like camels?[2] From then on, he never did anything unless someone was watching. In fourth grade, he told his teacher,

"Robin Hood couldn't boil Tuck because he wasn't a friar."[3] His fifth grade teacher commented that, "If Jay spent as much time studying as he does trying to be a comedian, he'd be a big star."[4] The rest is history.

Leno grew up near Andover, Massachusetts and got a speech therapy degree from Emerson College, where he then started a comedy club. A big, sweet guy with a protruding chin, he began his career in nightclubs, where he worked 300 nights a year before hitting it big with his own late-night talk show. Leno met his wife, Mavis, while performing at a comedy club in Los Angeles. She laughed at all his jokes at the right time.

Now retired from late-night television, Leno has more time to spend on his passion: his car collection. He owns at least 130 cars and 93 motorcycles.[5] At one point, he owned about 886 vehicles. Leno's collection ranges from old and new supercars, to American muscle cars, electric and steam-powered cars to a line of British cars and a collection of American cars from the late 1940s. His criteria for adding to his collection: cars he wants to drive.[6] He is fascinated with the mechanical and historical details of each machine, and he works on them himself.

Leno has a website called "Jay Leno's Garage," which contains video clips and photos of his automobiles. He has a column in *Popular Mechanics* that features his car collection and his advice. Leno also reviews high-end sports cars in humorous articles for *The L.A. Sunday Times*.

For nearly twenty years, Leno has been the grand marshal for the Love Ride, a motorcycle charity event that has raised nearly $14 million for charities such as muscular dystrophy and autism. Leno also auctioned his Fiat 500, which was sold for $385,000, to help wounded war veterans recover by providing them temporary housing.

Surely, Leno was an auto mechanic, perhaps a chauffeur or even a car designer in other lifetimes. And surely, he was a court jester or comedic entertainer in several lives.

Summary

* * *

Patterns of Celebrity Past Lives

M any of the fifty entertainers discussed in this book were fascinated by, if not passionate and committed to, entertaining from the time they were youngsters. LeAnn Rimes was singing in her highchair, tap dancing at two, and wanted to be a big star at five. As a tot, Meryl Davis was ice-skating competitively. Jennifer Lopez was dancing and singing at five as well. After winning the national tap dancing contest at the age of twelve, Catherine Zeta-Jones convinced her parents to let her move to London to act in plays. Magician Mat Franco was deciphering magic tricks from videos at four.

Keira Knightley begged for her own agent at three, thought she should earn her own living at six, and got her first TV role at seven. Kanye West was rapping, drawing, and writing poetry in third grade. Kevin Spacey snuck downstairs to mimic celebrities on TV, while Reese Witherspoon was taking adult acting classes at nine. Helen Mirren knew she wanted to be a traditional actress at six; Nicole Kidman did at three. Colin Firth's first acting experience was in infant's school at five. Robert De Niro liked to read plays as a child. At ten, he was the Cowardly Lion in *The Wizard of Oz*.

As a child, Ellen DeGeneres was helping amuse her mom through a divorce, and Jay Leno kept his family and classmates laughing at four. The young Billy Crystal kept his family entertained in their living room. Matt Damon role-played as his own form of therapy, while Ben Affleck wanted to be an actor for as long as he could remember and made home movies with his brother.

Richard Gere was composing music for high school productions. Liam Neeson got his first lead role in grade school because of his romantic attraction to the leading lady. Getting a guitar at twelve inspired Johnny Depp to become a rock musician. The siblings who could never remember a time when they weren't dancing, Julianne Hough and her older brother Derek were sent to England for formal training when Julianne was only ten.

At fourteen, Jennifer Lawrence dragged her parents to New York on spring break where an agent discovered her. Her "cold read" was impressive enough to open doors. At eleven, Taylor Swift roped her mother into driving to Nashville while she passed out demos to record companies. Kate Winslet pounced on her dad, an actor, at the beach, to convince him to let her go to drama school at eleven. At thirteen, West convinced his mother to let him record a rap song he had written.

One of the most significant clues to past lives, especially in the case of these outstanding celebrities, is what they did as children, how they spent their time, and how they expressed their passions and beliefs. Why were Zeta-Jones and the Hough siblings dancing up a storm, Franco practicing magic, while West was rapping at such young ages?

Past-life researcher Ian Stevenson found that children often play at, or show interest in, what they have done for a profession in a former life. Stevenson studied children in India who, he believed, were teachers and auto mechanics in past lives and who created these activities in their play.[1] Of course, in the case of the fifty celebrities in this book, the activities of these youngsters far transcended the limits of play.[1]

As for the celebrities who exhibited propensities towards performing before the age of six, regression therapist Dr. Bruce Goldberg has a theory. He explains that for the first few years of a child's life, his/her skull has small openings that may allow the soul or subconscious mind to escape and communicate directly with the child. This, he postulates, allows the child to bring past-life memories into conscious awareness.[2] Past-life believers, then, could apply Goldberg's theory to the celebrities in this book, celebrities who as young children displayed talents they likely brought forward from past lives.

As youngsters, many of these celebrities were passionate, even obsessed, about developing their talents and their futures. Why did they follow through on lessons while their peers were watching TV or playing computer games? Both Stevenson and Goldberg offer insight: they did so because they carried in their souls their passions from past lives.

Swift has been referred to as a child prodigy. How could Rimes sing before she could talk? How could Julianne Hough become the youngest dancer to win the International World Latin Championship at fifteen? In addition to persistence, follow through, and rigorous training, innate natural abilities shine through in many performers because of the past-life talents they bring with them into this lifetime.

These artists clearly demonstrated talent and knowledge beyond experience at a young age. Edgar Cayce believed that such abilities were developed and refined over lifetimes. He indicated that it took about 33 lifetimes to become a child prodigy. That would translate into 33 lifetimes dedicated to dancing, singing, and entertaining for Swift, Rimes and Hough. Even the business savvy that Swift and Rimes demonstrated early on in their careers is surely beyond their experience and training in this lifetime.

Hunger Games cast member Donald Sutherland compared Lawrence to famed actor Lawrence Olivier. Even the film's director said that she makes her acting look "effortless." Lawrence, who had never had an acting class, is a natural. This ability to have a talent come easily and naturally may be a strong indicator of past-life work.

Knowledge and talent beyond experience is another past-life clue. Knowledge and talent beyond experience just doesn't apply to youngsters. Meryl Streep has a photographic memory and a natural aptitude for speaking a variety of accents. Did those skills develop in this one lifetime, or has she refined them over lives and lives?

Although Renée Zellweger had never taken a dancing or singing class before, she received award nominations for her role in the musical film *Chicago*. Zellweger said she learned by watching co-star Zeta-Jones and being seriously coached.

And how come Depp was so adept at swordsmanship when he performed as Jack Sparrow? The swordmaster for one of his pirate roles said that Depp's ability to pick up the sword was as good as you could get.

In addition to early obsessions with performing and natural talents, another fascinating aspect that emerged while exploring celebrities' lives for this book was that the majority of the actors' parents were not in show business. Of the few who do have family members in the industry, they of course were assisted in their careers. Winslet's father was a stage actor, as was her mother and uncle, and her grandparents ran a repertory theatre. Knightley's father also was an actor, and her mother was a playwright. Those two women's families had a hand in helping their souls express themselves. Because Sandra Bullock was a "stage kid" for her German opera-singing mother, she appeared in an opera in Germany and was given music and ballet lessons at five.

Russell Crowe got his first role in a TV series at six, and probably learned how to act by osmosis, because he hung around movie shoots while his parents catered for them. By age seven, Angelina Jolie had acted in one of her father Jon Voight's movies. By eleven, she began studying at the Lee Strasbourg Theatre Institute where her mother, a French actress, had also studied. With both parents in acting, Benedict Cumberbatch began to act in boarding school, excelled at it, and pursued it to ultimately find himself an Academy Award nominee. Interestingly, even though Gary Sinese is the son of a film editor, he credits his interest in acting to his high school drama teacher.

Some proponents of past lives believe that we return to earth after having chosen our parents, life lessons, and circumstances. Choosing these parents may have led to opportunities and training that were necessary for the career growth of these individuals. Perhaps it's more a case of right place, right time, or, right parents rather than talents passed down through genetic memory.

Sometimes, having a parent in show business can be a double-edged sword. Even though George Clooney was in a family filled with movie stars, media personalities, and a beauty pageant winner, and at five had appeared on his father's talk shows, he initially decided to be a broadcast journalist so he wouldn't be compared to his father. Of course he didn't finish his degree, and instead he took a small film role from a relative and moved to Hollywood. And while Daniel Day-Lewis' mother was an actress and his grandfather the head of Ealing Studios, he might have been a cabinetmaker if he would have been selected for an apprenticeship. Film star Kirk Douglas tried to discourage his son Michael from acting. His son reacted by taking roles that were the polar opposite of the macho roles his father had played.

A few of the celebrities' parents even tried to discourage their children from acting. Mirren was one. Lopez was another. In fact, Lopez moved out after her parents insisted that performing was a stupid idea and that no Latinos did that. Perhaps choosing these parents brought about another set of skills or, ultimately, a strong level of confidence and self trust in Mirren's and Lopez's self-chosen goals.

Imagine the inner conviction of eighteen-year-old Lopez who must have believed on a soul level that she was destined for fame, so much so that she was convinced that she had to leave her parents' home in order to follow her destiny. On some level, perhaps because of her confidence from performing in other lives and her inner knowing of drawing on those talents, she could claim her destiny as she outshone 11,000 competitors to win the movie role of her life.

Why have some of these stars believed so strongly in their dreams since a young age? They believed enough to keep taking classes, for example. Some of them believed enough to drag their parents to New York or uproot their families to Nashville or Hollywood. Others believed enough even to return to a city and try to make it again and again.

This begs the question, are certain people born to fame? Perhaps. But the larger picture could be that it's not random and that individuals have developed their talents from lifetimes of commitment. Those who experience closed doors, come back for more because they are confident of their destinies.

Another past-life clue that past-life researchers point to is the course of education people choose, as well as their life vocations. In some of American psychic Cayce's life readings, he counseled youngsters and adults to develop certain career paths that would enhance the skills they had developed in other lives. In a reading for a six-month-old boy, for example, he reviewed a French lifetime in which the subject had worked with disease. He predicted that as the child grew, he would be interested in medicine. Cayce was right: as predicted, the boy had a paper route at ten to save for medical school tuition.[3]

Many of the celebrities in this book were first exposed to acting at school. As a high school senior, Spacey played Captain Von Trapp in *The Sound of Music*. Tom Hanks, Sinese and Mirren also began acting in high school. It wasn't until college that Zellweger, Denzel Washington, Jeff Daniels and Tommy Lee Jones began acting. They all completed their degrees. Brad Pitt acted in fraternity shows and quit college just credits shy of his journalism degree. Gere opted out of college to play the lead in *Grease* in London. First aspiring to become a physician, Jennifer Garner discovered her passion for acting and then changed her college major.

Thus far, I've listed early obsessions, natural talents, parents' roles, and education all as providing clues to one's past lives. Synchronicity is another past-life indicator. Both Streep and Matthew McConaughey had synchronistic events that led to redirecting their careers into acting. While both were in college, they had planned to be lawyers. Streep missed her appointment for acceptance into law school and refocused on acting, while McConaughey read a self-help book that gave him the courage to study film instead. An extraordinary synchronicity was when Rimes fished a song that had been written for Patsy Cline out of the trash. "Blue" became Rimes' first hit.

What, then, about lucky breaks? McConaughey got his first role after meeting a casting director in a Texas bar. Leonardo DiCaprio got his big break when he mouthed off to De Niro during a casting call with 400 other boys. De

Niro got a break when he hit it off with Martin Scorsese at a party in their Little Italy neighborhood. Were these events coincidences or were they synchronicity (meaningful experiences that weren't intentionally created)? Were these meetings predestined to happen? Were De Niro, DiCaprio and McConaughey meant to be famous because they had been actors before? Had they known their mentors in the past? Was destiny intentionally placing them on a fast track to success? Whether you call it a lucky break or synchronicity, being at the right place at the right time and easily winning someone over may offer a past-life clue.

Strong feelings about someone you've just met or love at first sight is another clue that you've known someone in a past life. It could be a result of an instant recognition and comfort level of a past-life relationship. Depp fell in love the moment he saw French actress Vanessa Paradis and quickly moved to France to start his life with her. Zeta-Jones called it love at first sight when she met Douglas on the movie set of *Zorro*. Robert Duvall had a similar experience in an Argentine bakery. Today, that woman is his wife and they share a home in, among other places, Argentina. Damon also experienced love at first sight with his wife Luciana Barroso, another Argentinean who he met when she was bartending in Miami. The pair enjoys a family life in Southern California. Because of their love at first sight experiences, it's highly likely that all these couples have known each other in their past lives.

Major friendships may also stem from other time periods. Damon and Affleck were pals since childhood, playing baseball together and nurturing each other's acting dreams. They grew up just blocks from each other and their families now live just blocks apart. Together, they have achieved international fame at the Oscars as co-writers for *Good Will Hunting*.

As for groups coming back together, Damon, Clooney and Pitt could easily have been past-life colleagues since they have worked together on several movies, played together and donated to the same causes. Perhaps this is what some past life scholars call "group karma" where all parties are committed to helping humanity on a global level and raising the geopolitical consciousness. It's even possible that they could have been in World War II together and committed to a common goal, such as the Allies' winning of the war.

Sometimes, actors and actresses who are cast together may have worked together in a past life as well. Firth has joked that Kidman is his "work wife" since they have been in at least four films together. Not only could this be probable, but also it incorporates a past-life clue: pay attention to the jokes people make. By repackaging truth as humor, controversial issues are more acceptable to our conscious mind. Perhaps Firth was unwittingly accessing his unconscious and tapping into a hidden truth.

So jokes are sometimes no laughing matter, and being cast in certain historic time periods or historic roles repeatedly could be a past-life clue for performers as well. As for a keen interest in a historic time period, British-born Day-Lewis was interested in the wild west of the U.S. He loves the old westerns. While cast in *The Last of The Mohicans*, he carried a rifle, camped, hunted animals, and built a canoe. Michigander Daniels is a Civil War buff, thus it's no surprise that he was cast as Union Colonel Joshua Chamberlain for both TV and film. Mirren was cast as British queens six times, while Hanks not only acted in the drama *Saving Private Ryan* but also produced several World War II miniseries.

As for geographical areas or settings, some Civil War skirmishes were fought on Duvall's Virginia property. Duvall even played his own ancestor, Confederate General Robert E. Lee in an epic Civil War movie, which was filmed on his beloved land. He also feels at home in Buenos Aires. Both McConaughey and Bullock live on ranches, while De Niro comes alive in the cafes of New York. Kevin Spacey feels at home in London; Depp does in France.

Kim Kardashian and West took their wedding party on a private tour of Versailles and held their wedding in a historical landmark overlooking Florence. Mirren and her husband got married in a Scottish castle. Day-Lewis, who feels like a traitor because he's British, identifies on a soul level with the West Region of Ireland. He loves the wild landscape and even the locals' accents. These locations, even accents and other languages, can serve as past-life triggers for us. Jolie had such an affinity for Cambodia that she adopted her son Maddox from Cambodia, has set up a school there, and believes that she was a past-life Buddhist monk at Angor Wat, the largest religious temple in the world.

Even though she doesn't speak German, Cate Blanchett had a dream of performing in Berlin. Years later, she portrayed a Jewish woman married to a German SS officer in Berlin at the end of the War. Sometimes, dreams can be a good outlet for remembering past lives.

Being repeatedly cast in geographic areas or settings, again, provides past-life clues. Hanks has been stranded at sea three times and captured by pirates once. Clint Eastwood had a string of American-made western movies. He's played cowpokes, drifters, and deputies. Like John Wayne, Eastwood most likely was a cowboy before.

If someone is particularly drawn to art or artifacts, that could be another past-life clue. Eastwood collects western art. Hanks has collected over eighty typewriters. Witherspoon collects old embroidery. Knightley bought herself an English dollhouse of the mansion inspired from the book *Pride and Prejudice*. At one point, Leno owned about 886 vehicles; some of them even dated back to the late 1940s. In each case, each artifact category is likely an indicator to a particular past life.

An interest in specific dance, music, or fashion could also be a past-life indicator. Duvall has a passion for tango music and dancing the tango. As for an interest in fashion, Depp is a great example. As a teenager in a band, Depp wore his mother's crushed velvet shirts with French sleeves and seersucker bell-bottoms. He lusted after platform shoes. While playing a pirate, he wanted lots of gold-capped teeth and, even after filming, wore a skull ring and a pirate tattoo. Eastwood wore the same boots he had worn in the TV series *Rawhide*, in his first and last Westerns. They are now part of his private collection. British actress Mirren is said to have a tattoo of a star on her left hand that she acquired on a Native American reservation; it is believed to be a Native American symbol.

As for hobbies, Affleck and Damon have been serious gamblers. Crystal and Clooney love baseball. Gere played lacrosse, which traces its roots to the Native Americans. Jones is an avid polo player and has homes in two polo meccas. Day-Lewis is a cobbler. Again, these hobbies offer more past-life clues.

Preferences, such as a philosophical leaning, could be a significant past-life clue as well. Although Gere was raised Methodist, he has been practicing Buddhism since his twenties, has traveled to Nepal, and has supported a free Tibet and the Dalai Lama. Cumberbatch took a year off school to teach English in a Tibetan monastery and subscribes to Buddhism, like Gere. Jolie, too, could have been Buddhist in a former life.

In stark contrast, what could be described as a clearly unenlightened philosophical attitude that could have been a past-life carry-over, is the behavior of former LA Clippers basketball team owner Donald Sterling. His team ownership was taken away from him as the result of racially prejudiced comments. His manager had compared Sterling's leadership style to that of a plantation atmosphere. Certainly this suggests a past life of Sterling's.

Author and parapsychologist Gina Cerminara reported that in a trance, Cayce said, "we are the sum total of all our past life memories. We manifest them in habits, idiosyncrasies, likes and dislikes, talents, blind spots, physical and emotional strengths, and vulnerabilities."[4] Patterns also recur from lifetime to lifetime.

Foremost reincarnation researcher Dr. Stevenson found that of the approximately 1200 cases of children's past-life memories he validated, in ten percent of the cases gender was reversed.[5] Some reincarnationists believe that the soul contains both male and female characteristics, and we experience male and female lives to more fully express both qualities. These past-life tendencies are expressed as our current degree of masculinity or femininity. Proclivities to homosexuality may have its roots in a past life. In those cases, some of the sexual traits and preferences of the other sex could come forward in the current life, confusing desires and impulses.[6] Given this, it could be possible that DeGeneres, an outspoken advocate of homosexuality who feels comfortable in suits and blue sneakers, was a male in her immediate past life or lives. Perhaps she still carries memories, even genetic, of male lives and is in a period of adjustment and integration.

Besides sexual preferences, personality traits and other types of patterns can recur or influence certain modern-day thoughts, feelings, or actions. DiCaprio has spoken previously of being hesitant to make a commitment to marry. Perhaps the subconscious memory of the loss of a wife or loved one in a prior life might influence his inability to make a commitment. And although McConaughey was the catch of his class, he was a loner growing up, and he loves to go solo on exotic adventures. He probably had many adventuresome but lonely past lives. This lifetime, even as an eight year old, what he wanted more than anything was to be a father.

He revels in his family life, and such an affinity coupled with his strong desire to travel solo might suggest that he lost his family in a previous lifetime.

Streep also prioritizes her husband and family as of utmost importance. Perhaps Streep experienced many lifetimes of performing achievement, but had to give up having a family. This time, she has both a family and a remarkable career.

Being consistently typecast in roles like spiritual teacher or victim can also point to an actor's past life. Neeson has been cast as a wise mentor in roles such as the Jedi Master in *Star Wars*. In casting him, director George Lucas perceived Neeson's strength of character and qualities of spiritual leadership. Those characteristics, most likely, were developed in other lifetimes. In many of her roles, Zellweger plays a woman who is helpless, desperate, and victimized. In her current life, Zellweger's dream was to become self-sufficient. She has far exceeded her initial, but powerful goal and has moved on from past struggles.

Physical reactions, emotions, and sensations can wake up our past-life memories as well. While during a romantic interlude from filming with his wife, Damon discovered he had a fear of heights. Such a reaction or phobia usually means a past-life death from falling. While filming *Sophie's Choice*, for which Streep won her first Academy Award for Best Actress, Streep refused to redo the scene where she has to choose between giving away her son or daughter. She found the concentration camp scene too gut-wrenching. Again, like Damon, this reaction suggests a past life experience. Playing disabled and suicidal Lt. Dan in *Forrest Gump* triggered strong emotions in Sinise and was the catalyst for his life's work. Following the film, Sinise has consistently supported returning vets with ongoing band performances and organizations he started for their aid. Such emotional connections indicate a possible past-life connection.

Finally, movies such as *Railway Man* and *Unbroken* may be able to help heal the actors and actresses who perform in them, those who may have lived through similar circumstances or traumatic events in their own past lives. As Jolie says, "the roles I choose are my therapy." At the same time, these movies, with a message of forgiveness, or a message of insight into humanity and life lessons learned, can help to raise the collective consciousness and heal the wounds of viewers and others who may have experienced similar traumas, both in past lives and in present time.

Entertainment and entertainers can and should be used to their maximum potential: to entertain, inform, and uplift. If our mass karma can be expedited, so much the better! If viewers who are touched by a performance can be encouraged on their soul's journey or have their own load lifted, even for two hours, that is an ultimate gift on many levels.

Through observing the possible past lives of these accomplished entertainers, we have glimpsed them as multidimensional beings and peered into a window into their souls. In doing so, we have gained the skills to peer further into our own. It is my hope that you will continue to attune to past-life clues as you journey through this life. May you open up to the complexities within every being, those in the limelight, those next door, and those within you.

Endnotes

Throughout this book, references have been made to the author's three previously published books initially published by A.R.E. Press and currently available on Amazon.com and other retailers:

16 Clues to Your Past Lives: A Guide to Discovering Who You Were by Barbara Lane, 1999

Echoes from the Battlefield: First Person Accounts of Civil War Past Lives by Barbara Lane, 1996

Echoes from Medieval Halls: Past-Life Memories from the Middle Ages by Barbara Lane, 1997

Preface: The Continuing Integration of Science, Consciousness, Time, and Reincarnation

[1] "IONS Directory Profile: Edgar D. Mitchell, ScD." In *Ions: Institute of Noetic Sciences.* Retrieved 10 October 2014 from / www.ions.org/directory/person/edgar-mitchell.

[2] "Conservation of Energy." In *Wikipedia: The Free Encyclopedia.* Retrieved 10 May 2014 from http://en.wikipedia.org/wiki/Conservation_of_energy.

[3] Ibid.

[4] "Stephen Hawking." In *Wikipedia: The Free Encyclopedia.* Retrieved 12 May 2014 from http://en.wikipedia.org/wiki/Stephen_Hawking.

[5] "Do You Only Live Once?" In *Robert Lanza, M.D.— Biocentrism.* Retrieved 12 May 2014 from http://www.robert-lanza-biocentrism.com/do-you-only-live-once/.

[6] Ibid.

[7] Ibid.

[8] "Can Our Memories Survive the Death of Our Brains?" by Rupert Sheldrake. In *What Survives? Contemporary Explorations of Life After Death*, ed. Gary Doore. pp. 111-121; see also *The*

Rebirth of Nature: The Greening of Science and God by Rupert Sheldrake.

[9] *Quantum Healing* by Deepak Chopra, M.D., p 87.

[10] "'Life before Life' with Jim Tucker." In IONS Library: Audio Teleseminars. Retrieved 15 May 2014 from http://www.noetic.org.

[11] *Reincarnation in World Thought* by Joseph Head and S.L. Cranston, p. 10.

[12] "Reincarnation." In *Wikipedia: The Free Encyclopedia*. Retrieved 12 May 2014 from http://en.wikipedia.org/wiki/Reincarnation.

[13] *Reincarnation in World Thought* by Joseph Head and S.L. Cranston.

[14] *Edgar Cayce on Reincarnation* by Noel Langely, pp.179-201.

[15] "Albert Einstein." In *Wikipedia: The Free Encyclopedia*. Retrieved 10 May 2014 from http://en.wikipedia.org/wiki/Albert_Enstein.

Introduction: Unearthing Celebrity Past-Life Clues

[1] *Child Star: An Autobiography* by Shirley Temple Black.

[2] *Many Mansions* by Gina Cerminara, p.89.

Chapter 1: Meryl Streep

[1] "Meryl Streep." In *Wikipedia: The Free Encyclopedia*. Retrieved 27 September 2014 from http://en. wikipedia.org/wiki/Meryl_Streep.

[2] Ibid.

[3] "Meryl Streep." In *The Internet Movie Database*. Retrieved 27 September 2014 from http://www.imdb.com/name/nm0000658/.

[4] Ibid.

[5] Ibid.
[6] Ibid.
[7] "Meryl Streep." In *Wikipedia: The Free Encyclopedia.* Retrieved 27 September 2014 from http://en. wikipedia.org/wiki/ Meryl_Streep.
[8] Ibid.

Chapter 2: Nicole Kidman

[1] "The Actress Opens Up about Her Adventurous, Love-Filled Life" by Lauren Waterman. In *Elle*, January 2014, p. 155.
[2] Ibid. p 155.
[3] Ibid. p 116.
Also Consulted:
"Nicole Kidman." In *The Internet Movie Database.* Retrieved 4 June 2014 from http://www.imdb.com/ name/nm0000173.
"Nicole Kidman." In *Wikipedia: The Free Encyclopedia.* Retrieved 4 June 2014 from http://en.wikipedia.org/wiki/ Nicole_Kidman.
"Nicole Kidman." In *People.* Retrieved 4 June 2014 from http://www.people.com/people/nicole_kidman/ biography/ ed_ Julia_Wang.
"Railway Man." In *Wikipedia: The Free Encyclopedia.* Retrieved 4 June 2014 from http://en.wikipedia.org/wiki/The_Railway_ Man_(film).

Chapter 3: Colin Firth

[1] "Railway Man." In *Wikipedia: The Free Encyclopedia.* Retrieved 6 June 2014 from http://en.wikipedia.org/wiki/ The_Railway_Man_(film).
Also Consulted:

"Colin Firth." In *Wikipedia: The Free Encyclopedia.* Retrieved 6 June 2014 from http://en.wikipedia.org/wiki/Colin_Firth.
"Colin Firth." In *The Internet Movie Database.* Retrieved 6 June 2014 from http://www.imdb.com/name/ nm0000147/.
"Colin Firth." In *The Biography.* Retrieved 6 June 2014 from http://www.biography.com/people.colin-firth0000147/.

Chapter 4: Robert De Niro

[1] "Robert De Niro." In *The Internet Movie Database.* Retrieved 8 June 2014 from http://www.imdb.com/name/nm0000134/.
[2] Ibid.
[3] Ibid.
Also Consulted:
"Robert De Niro." In *Wikipedia: The Free Encyclopedia.* Retrieved 8 June 2014 from http://en.wikipedia.org/wiki/ Robert_De_Niro.
"Remembering the Artist Robert De Niro, Sr." In *HBO: Documentaries.* Retrieved 8 June 2014 from http://www. hbo.com/documentaries/remembering-the-artist-robert-de-niro-sr#/.
"Robert De Niro." In *Rotten Tomatoes.* Retrieved 8 June 2014 from http://www.rottentomatoes.com/celebrity/robert_de_niro/biography/ed.

Chapter 5: Billy Crystal

[1] "Billy Crystal 700 Sundays." In *HBO: Comedy.* Retrieved 12 June 2014 from http://www.hbo.com/comedy/billy-crystal-700-sundays#/.
[2] "Billy Crystal." In *The Internet Movie Database.* Retrieved 12 June 2014 from http://www.imdb.com/ name/nm0000345/.
Also Consulted:

"Billy Crystal." In *Wikipedia: The Free Encyclopedia*. Retrieved 12 June 2014 from http://en.wikipedia.org/wiki/Billy_Crystal.

Chapter 6: Jon Favreau

[1] "Soul Food" by Glen Starkey. In *New Times San Luis Obispo*, June 5, 2014.
[2] Ibid.
Also Consulted:
"Jon Favreau." In *The Internet Movie Database*. Retrieved 20 June 2014 from http://www.imdb.com/name/ nm0269463/.
"Jon Favreau." In *Wikipedia: The Free Encyclopedia*. Retrieved 20 June 2014 from http://en.wikipedia.org/wiki/Jon_Favreau.

Chapter 7: Russell Crowe

[1] "Russell Crowe." In *The Internet Movie Database*. Retrieved 23 June 2014 from http://www.imdb.com/ name/nm0000128/.
[2] Ibid.
[3] "Russell Crowe." In *Wikipedia: The Free Encyclopedia*. Retrieved 23 June 2014 from http://en.wikipedia.org/wiki/ Russell_Crowe.
[4] "Russell Crowe." In *The Internet Movie Database*. Retrieved 23 June 2014 from http://www.imdb.com/name/nm0000128/.
[5] "Russell Crowe." In *Wikipedia: The Free Encyclopedia*. Retrieved 23 June 2014 from http://en.wikipedia.org/wiki/ Russell_Crowe.
Also Consulted:
"Russell Crowe." In *Rotten Tomatoes*. Retrieved 23 June 2014 from http://www.rottentomatoes.com/ celebrity/ russell_crowe/biography.

Chapter 8: Robert Duvall

[1] "Robert Duvall." In *Wikipedia: The Free Encyclopedia.* Retrieved 6 July 2014 from http://en.wikipedia.org/ wiki/ Robert_Duvall.

[2] Ibid.

[3] Ibid.

[4] "Robert Duvall." In *The Internet Movie Database.* Retrieved 6 July 2014 from http://www.imdb.com/name/nm0000380/.

[5] Ibid.

[6] Ibid.

Also Consulted:

"Robert Duvall." In *Rotten Tomatoes.* Retrieved 6 July 2014 from http://www.rottentomatoes.com/ celebrity/robert_duvall/ biography.

Chapter 9: Donald Sterling

[1] "Donald Sterling." In *Wikipedia: The Free Encyclopedia.* Retrieved 9 July 2014 from http://en.wikipedia. org/wiki/ Donald_Sterling.

[2] "Donald Sterling." In *Forbes.* Retrieved 25 July 2014 from http://www.forbes.com/sites/ mikeozanian/2014/05/31/ how-donald-sterling-and-v-stiviano-turned-the-90-billion-sports-industry-on-its-head/.

[3] "Donald Sterling." In *Wikipedia: The Free Encyclopedia.* Retrieved 9 July 2014 from http://en.wikipedia. org/wiki/ Donald_Sterling.

[4] Ibid.

[5] "Donald Sterling." In *Forbes.* Retrieved 25 July 2014 from http://www.forbes.com/sites/mikeozanian /2014/05/31/ how-donald-sterling-and-v-stiviano-turned-the-90-billion-sports-industry-on-its-head/.

Chapter 10: Johnny Depp

[1] "Johnny Depp." In *Wikipedia: The Free Encyclopedia.* Retrieved 27 July 2014 from http://en.wikipedia.org/wiki/Johnny_Depp.

[2] "Johnny Depp." In *The Internet Movie Database.* Retrieved 27 July 2014 from http://www.imdb.com/ name/nm0000136/.

[3] "Johnny Depp." In *Wikipedia: The Free Encyclopedia.* Retrieved 27 July 2014 from http://en.wikipedia.org/wiki/Johnny_Depp.

[4] "Johnny Depp." In *The Internet Movie Database.* Retrieved 27 July 2014 from http://www.imdb.com/ name/nm0000136/.

[5] Ibid.

[6] "Island I Do's" by Brody Brown and Charles Thorp. In *US Magazine*, February 16, 2015, p. 46.

[7] "Johnny Depp & Amber Heard: Wedding Bells!" by Melody Chiu. In *People*, February 25, 2015, p. 28.

Also Consulted:

"Johnny Depp." In *Biography.* Retrieved 27 July 2014 from http://www.biography.com/people/johnny-depp-9542522.

Chapter 11: Kim Kardashian & Kanye West

[1] "Belvedere." In *Wikipedia: The Free Encyclopedia.* Retrieved 1 August 2014 from http://en.wikipedia. org/wiki/Belvedere_(fort).

[2] "Kim Kardashian Wedding Dress Photo." In *People Magazine.* Retrieved 1 August 2014 from http://www.people.com/article/kim-kardashian-wedding-dress-photo-2014-kanye-west.

[3] "Palace of Versailles." In *Wikipedia: The Free Encyclopedia.* Retrieved 1 August 2014 from http://en.wikipedia.org/wiki/Palace_of_Versailles.

Also Consulted:

"Kim Kardashian." In *Wikipedia: The Free Encyclopedia.* Retrieved 1 August 2014 from http://en.wikipedia.org/wiki/Kim_Kardashian.

"Kim Kardashian." In *The Internet Movie Database.* Retrieved 1 August 2014 from http://www.imdb.com/ name/ nm2578007/.

"Kanye West." In *Wikipedia: The Free Encyclopedia.* Retrieved 1 August 2014 from http://en.wikipedia.org/wiki/Kanye_West.

"Kanye West." In *The Internet Movie Database.* Retrieved 1 August 2014 from http://www.imdb.com/kanye-west/ nm1577190/.

Chapter 12: Derek & Julianne Hough

[1] "Julianne Hough." In *The Internet Movie Database.* Retrieved 10 August 2014 from http://www.imdb.com/name/nm2584600/.

[2] Ibid.

[3] Ibid.

[4] "Julianne Hough." In *Wikipedia: The Free Encyclopedia.* Retrieved 10 August 2014 from http://en.wikipedia.org/wiki/Julianne_Hough.

Also Consulted:

"Growing Up Hough!" by Mia McNiece. In *People,* June 30, 2014, pp. 54-58.

"Derek Hough." In *Wikipedia: The Free Encyclopedia.* Retrieved 10 August 2014 from http://en.wikipedia.org/wiki/Derek_Hough.

"Derek Hough." In *The Internet Movie Database.* Retrieved 10 August 2014 from http://www.imdb.com/ name/ nm2625538/.

Chapter 13: Kevin Spacey

[1] "Kevin Spacey." In *The Internet Movie Database*. Retrieved 19 August 2014 from http://www.imdb.com/ name/ nm0000228/.

[2] Ibid.

[3] Ibid.

[4] Ibid.

Also Consulted:

"Kevin Spacey." In *Wikipedia: The Free Encyclopedia*. Retrieved 1 August 2014 from http://en.wikipedia.org/wiki/ Kevin_Spacey.

Chapter 14: Tom Hanks

[1] "Tom Hanks." In *The Internet Movie Database*. Retrieved 23 August 2014 from http://www.imdb.com/name/ nm0000158/.

[2] "Tom Hanks." In *Wikipedia: The Free Encyclopedia*. Retrieved 23 August 2014 from http://en.wikipedia.org/wiki/ Tom_Hanks.

[3] "Tom Hanks." In *The Internet Movie Database*. Retrieved 23 August 2014 from http://www.imdb.com/name/ nm0000158/.

[4] Ibid.

[5] Ibid.

[6] Ibid.

[7] Ibid.

Chapter 15: Gary Sinise

[1] "Gary Sinise." In *The Internet Movie Database.* Retrieved 29 August 2014 from http://www.imdb.com/name/nm0000158/.

[2] "Gary Sinise." In *Wikipedia: The Free Encyclopedia.* Retrieved 29 August 2014 from http://en.wikipedia.org/wiki/Gary_Sinise.

[3] Ibid.

Chapter 16: Meryl Davis

[1] "Meryl Davis." In *Wikipedia: The Free Encyclopedia.* Retrieved 4 September 2014 from http://en.wikipedia.org/wiki/Meryl_Davis.

[2] "Maxim Chmerkovskiy Admits Relationship with Meryl Davis is Real." In *The Stir.* Retrieved September 2013 from http://thestir.cafemom.com/entertainment/173846/maksim_chmerkovskiy_admits_relationship_with.

[3] Ibid.

Also Consulted:

"Meryl Davis." In *The Internet Movie Database.* Retrieved 4 September 2014 from http://www.imdb.com/name/nm3196485/.

Chapter 17: Clint Eastwood

[1] "Clint Eastwood." In *Wikipedia: The Free Encyclopedia.* Retrieved 7 September 2014 from http://en.wikipedia.org/wiki/Clint_Eastwood.

[2] Ibid.

[3] Ibid.

[4] "Clint Eastwood." In *The Internet Movie Database*. Retrieved 7 September 2014, from http://www.imdb.com/name/nm0000142/.
[5] Ibid.
[6] Ibid.
[7] Ibid.

Chapter 18: Jennifer Lopez

[1] "Jennifer Lopez." In *The Internet Movie Database*. Retrieved 10 September 2014 from *http://www.imdb.com/name/nm0000182/*.
[2] "Jennifer Lopez." In *Wikipedia: The Free Encyclopedia*. Retrieved 10 September 2014 from http://en.wikipedia.org/wiki/Jennifer_Lopez.
[3] 93 Ibid.
[4] 94 "Jennifer Lopez." In *The Internet Movie Database*. Retrieved 10 September 2014 from *http://www.imdb.com/*Ibid.
[5] "Jennifer Lopez." In *The Internet Movie Database*. Retrieved 10 September 2014 from *http://www.imdb.com/ name/nm0000182/*.

Chapter 19: Reese Witherspoon

[1] "Reese Witherspoon." In *Wikipedia: The Free Encyclopedia*. Retrieved 12 September 2014 from http://en. wikipedia.org/wiki/Reese_Witherspoon.
[2] Ibid.
[3] "Reese Witherspoon." In *The Internet Movie Database*. Retrieved 12 September 2014 from http://www.imdb.com/name/nm0000702/.
[4] "Reese Witherspoon." In *Wikipedia: The Free Encyclopedia*. Retrieved 12 September 2014 from http://en. wikipedia.org/wiki/Reese_Witherspoon.
[5] Ibid.

[6] Ibid.

[7] Ibid.

[8] "Reese Witherspoon." In *The Internet Movie Database.* Retrieved 12 September 2014 from http://www.imdb.com/name/nm0000702/.

[9] Ibid.

Chapter 20: Angelina Jolie

[1] "Angelina Jolie." In *Wikipedia: The Free Encyclopedia.* Retrieved 14 September 2014 from http://en.wikipedia.org/wiki/Angelina_Jolie.

[2] Ibid.

[3] "Angelina Jolie." In *The Internet Movie Database.* Retrieved 14 September 2014 from http://www.imdb.com/name/nm0001401/.

[4] "Angelina Jolie." In *Wikipedia: The Free Encyclopedia.* Retrieved 14 September 2014 from http://en.wikipedia.org/wiki/Angelina_Jolie.

[5] "Angelina Jolie." In *The Internet Movie Database.* Retrieved 14 September 2014 from http://www.imdb.com/ name/nm0001401/.

[6] "Angie: I Was A Buddhist Monk! In *InTouch Weekly,* Vol. 14, Issue 44. Nov 3, 2014, p.41.

[7] "Angelina Jolie." In *The Internet Movie Database.* from 14 September 2014 from http://www.imdb.com/name/nm0001401/.

[8] Ibid.

Also Consulted:

"Untamed Heart" by Hedi Slimane. In *Elle,* May 7, 2014, pp 204-205, 234, and 235.

Chapter 21: Brad Pitt

[1] "Brad Pitt." In *Wikipedia: The Free Encyclopedia.* Retrieved 16 September 2014 from http://en.wikipedia.org/wiki/Brad_Pitt.

[2] Ibid.

[3] "Brad Pitt." In *The Internet Movie Database.* Retrieved 18 September 2014 from http://www.imdb.com/ name/nm0000093/.

Chapter 22: Leonardo DiCaprio

[1] Leonardo DiCaprio." In *The Internet Movie Database.* Retrieved 22 September 2014 from http://www.imdb.com/name/nm0000138/.

[2] Ibid.

[3] "Leonardo DiCaprio." In *Wikipedia: The Free Encyclopedia.* Retrieved 22 September 2014 from http://en.wikipedia.org/wiki/Leonardo_DiCaprio.

[4] "Leonardo DiCaprio." In *The Internet Movie Database.* Retrieved 22 September 2014 from http://www.imdb.com/name/nm0000138/.

[5] Ibid.

Chapter 23: Helen Mirren

[1] "Helen Mirren." In *The Internet Movie Database.* Retrieved 25 September 2014 from http://www.imdb.com/name/nm0000545/.

[2] Ibid.

[3] Ibid.

[4] Ibid.

[5] "A Wise and Witty Dame" by David Hochman. In *AARP*, June-July 2014, pp. 31-33.
[6] "Helen Mirren." In *Wikipedia: The Free Encyclopedia*. Retrieved 25 September 2014 from http://en. wikipedia.org/ wiki/Helen_Mirren.

Chapter 24: Ben Affleck & Jennifer Garner

[1] "Ben Affleck." In *Wikipedia: The Free Encyclopedia*. Retrieved 29 September 2014 from http://en.wikipedia.org/wiki/ Ben_Affleck.
[2] Ibid.
[3] "Jennifer Garner." In *The Internet Movie Database*. Retrieved 29 September 2014 from http://www.imdb. com/name/ nm0004950/.
[4] "Ben Affleck." In *Wikipedia: The Free Encyclopedia*. Retrieved 29 September 2014 from http://en.wikipedia. org/wiki/ Ben_Affleck.
[5] "Ben Affleck." In *The Internet Movie Database*. Retrieved 29 September 2014 from http://www.imdb.com/name/ nm0000255/.
[6] Ibid.
[7] Ibid.

Chapter 25: George Clooney

[1] George Clooney." In *The Internet Movie Database*. Retrieved 30 September 2014 from http://www.imdb.com/name/ nm0000123/.
[2] Ibid.
[3] Ibid.
[4] Ibid.
[5] Ibid.

Also Consulted:
"George Clooney." In *Wikipedia: The Free Encyclopedia.*
Retrieved 30 September 2014 from http://en.wikipedia.org/
wiki/George_Clooney.

Chapter 26: Matt Damon

[1] "Matt Damon." In *Wikipedia: The Free Encyclopedia.* Retrieved
2 October 2014 from http://en.wikipedia.org/wiki/
Matt_Damon.
[2] "Matt Damon." In *The Internet Movie Database.* Retrieved
2 October 2014 from http://www.imdb.com/ name/
nm0000354/.
[3] Ibid.
[4] Ibid.
[5] Ibid.

Chapter 27: Catherine Zeta-Jones & Michael Douglas

[1] "Catherine Zeta-Jones." In *People.* Retrieved 4 October 2014
from http://www.people.com/people /catherine_zeta-jones/
biography/.
[2] "Catherine Zeta-Jones." In *The Internet Movie Database.*
Retrieved 4 October 2014 from http://www.imdb.com/
name/nm0001876/.
[3] Ibid.
[4] "Michael Douglas." In *The Internet Movie Database.* Retrieved
4 October 2014 from http://www.imdb.com/name/
nm0000140/.
[5] "Catherine Zeta-Jones." In *The Internet Movie Database.*
Retrieved 4 October 2014 from http://www.imdb.com/
name/nm0001876/.
[6] Ibid.

Also Consulted:

"Catherine Zeta-Jones." In *Wikipedia: The Free Encyclopedia*. Retrieved 4 October 2014 from http://en. wikipedia.org/ wiki/Catherine_Zeta-Jones.

"Michael Douglas." In *Wikipedia: The Free Encyclopedia*. Retrieved 4 October 2014 from http://en.wikipedia.org/ wiki/Michael_Douglas.

Chapter 28: Sandra Bullock

[1] "Sandra Bullock." In *The Internet Movie Database*. Retrieved 6 October 2014 from http://www.imdb.com/name/ nm0000113/.
[2] Ibid.
[3] Ibid.
[4] Ibid.
[5] Ibid.
[6] Ibid.
[7] Ibid.
Also Consulted:
"Sandra Bullock." In *Wikipedia: The Free Encyclopedia*. Retrieved 5 October 2014 from http://en.wikipedia.org/ wiki/Sandra_Bullock.

Chapter 29: Richard Gere

[1] "Richard Gere." In *The Internet Movie Database*. Retrieved 8 October 2014 from http://www.imdb.com/ name/ nm0000152/.
[2] Ibid.
Also Consulted:

"Richard Gere." In *Wikipedia: The Free Encyclopedia*. Retrieved 8 October 2014 from http://en.wikipedia. org/wiki/ Richard_Gere.

Chapter 30: Renée Zellweger

[1] "Renée Zellweger." In *Wikipedia: The Free Encyclopedia*. Retrieved 10 October 2014 from http://en. wikipedia.org/ wiki/Renee_Zellweger.
[2] "Renée Zellweger." In *The Internet Movie Database*. Retrieved 10 October 2014 from http://www.imdb.com/name/ nm0000250/.
[3] Ibid.

Chapter 31: Matthew McConaughey

[4] "Matthew McConaughey." In *The Internet Movie Database*. Retrieved 12 October 2014 from http://www.imdb.com/ name/nm0000190/.
[5] Ibid.
[6] "10 Moments that Changed My Life" by Matthew McConaughey. In *People*, November 17, 2014.
Also Consulted:
"Matthew McConaughey." In *Wikipedia: The Free Encyclopedia*. Retrieved 12 October 2014 from http://en.wikipedia.org/ wiki/Matthew_McConaughey.

Chapter 32: Denzel Washington

[1] "Denzel Washington." In *The Internet Movie Database*. Retrieved 14 October 2014 from http://www.imdb.com/ name/nm0000243/.

[2] "Denzel Washington." In *Wikipedia: The Free Encyclopedia.* Retrieved 12 October 2014 from http://en. wikipedia.org/wiki/Denzel_Washington.

Chapter 33: Jeff Daniels

[1] "Jeff Daniels." In *The Internet Movie Database.* Retrieved 17 October 2014 from http://www.imdb.com/ name/nm0001099.
[2] Ibid.
Also Consulted:
"Jeff Daniels." In *Wikipedia: The Free Encyclopedia.* Retrieved 17 October 2014 from http://en.wikipedia.org/wiki/Jeff_Daniels.

Chapter 34: Taylor Swift

[1] "Taylor Swift." In *Wikipedia: The Free Encyclopedia.* Retrieved 19 October 2014 from http://en.wikipedia.org/wiki/Taylor_Swift.
Also Consulted:
"Taylor Swift." In *The Internet Movie Database.* Retrieved 19 October 2014 from http://www.imdb.com/ name/nm2357847.
"Taylor Strikes a Chord: How Pop's Savviest Romantic Conquered the Music Business," by Jack Dickey. In *Time Magazine,* November 24, 2014, pp 42-48.

Chapter 35: Mat Franco

[1] "Mat Franco." In *Wikipedia: The Free Encyclopedia*. Retrieved 21 October 2014 from http://en.wikipedia.org/wiki/Mat_Franco.

Chapter 36: Tommy Lee Jones

[1] "Polo." In *Wikipedia: The Free Encyclopedia*. Retrieved 23 October 2014 from http://en.wikipedia.org/ wiki/Polo.
[2] "Tommy Lee Jones." In *The Internet Movie Database*. Retrieved 23 October 2014 from http://www.imdb. com/name/nm0000169.
Also Consulted:
"Tommy Lee Jones." In *Wikipedia: The Free Encyclopedia*. Retrieved 23 October 23 2014 from http://en. wikipedia. org/wiki/Tommy_Lee_Jones.

Chapter 37: Ellen DeGeneres

[1] "Ellen DeGeneres." In *The Internet Movie Database*. Retrieved 25 October 2014 from http://www.imdb. com/name/nm000112.
[2] Ibid.
Also Consulted:
"Ellen DeGeneres." In *Wikipedia: The Free Encyclopedia*. Retrieved 25 October 2014 from http://en.wikipedia.org/ wiki/Ellen_DeGeneres.

Chapter 38: Daniel Day-Lewis

[1] "Daniel Day-Lewis." In *Wikipedia: The Free Encyclopedia.* Retrieved 7 October 2014 from http://en.wikipedia.org/wiki/Daniel_Day-Lewis.

[2] "Daniel Day-Lewis." In *The Internet Movie Database.* Retrieved 27 October 2014 from http://www.imdb. com/name/nm0000358/.

[3] Ibid.

[4] Ibid.

[5] Ibid.

[6] Ibid.

[7] Ibid.

[8] Ibid.

[9] Ibid.

[10] Ibid.

Chapter 39: Cate Blanchett

[1] "Cate Blanchett." In *Wikipedia: The Free Encyclopedia.* Retrieved 29 October 2014 from http://en.wikipedia.org/wiki/Cate_Blanchett.

[2] "Cate Blanchett." In *The Internet Movie Database.* Retrieved 29 October 2014 from http://www.imdb. com/name/nm0000949.

[3] Ibid.

Chapter 40: Kate Winslet

[1] "Kate Winslet." In *The Internet Movie Database.* Retrieved 31 October 2014 from http://www.imdb. com/name/nm0000701/.

[2] Ibid.

[3] Ibid.
Also Consulted:
"Kate Winslet." In *Wikipedia: The Free Encyclopedia*. Retrieved 31 October 2014 from http://en.wikipedia.org/wiki/Kate_Winslet.

Chapter 41: Jennifer Lawrence

[1] "Jennifer Lawrence." In *The Internet Movie Database*. Retrieved 1 November 2014 from http://www.imdb.com/name/nm2225369.
[2] "Jennifer Lawrence." In *Wikipedia: The Free Encyclopedia*. Retrieved 1 November 2014 from http://en.wikipedia.org/wiki/Jennifer_Lawrence.
[3] Ibid.
[4] "Jennifer Lawrence." In *The Internet Movie Database*. Retrieved 1 November 2014 from http://www.imdb.com/name/nm2225369.

Chapter 42: Keira Knightley

[1] "Keira Knightley." In *Wikipedia: The Free Encyclopedia*. Retrieved 3 November 2014 from http://en.wikipedia.org/wiki/Keira_Knightley.
[2] Ibid.
Also Consulted:
"Keira Knightley." In *The Internet Movie Database*. Retrieved 3 November 2014 from http://www.imdb. com/name/nm0461136/.

Chapter 43: LeAnn Rimes

[1] "LeAnn Rimes." In *The Internet Movie Database.* Retrieved 5 November 2014 from http://www.imdb. com/name/nm0005361/.

[2] Ibid.

[3] "LeAnn Rimes." In *Wikipedia: The Free Encyclopedia.* Retrieved 5 November 2014 from http://en.wikipedia.org/wiki/LeAnn_Rimes.

[4] "LeAnn Rimes." In *The Internet Movie Database.* Retrieved 5 November 2014 from http://www.imdb.com/name/nm0005361/.

Chapter 44: Liam Neeson

[5] "Liam Neeson." In *Wikipedia: The Free Encyclopedia.* Retrieved 7 November 2014 from http://en.wikipedia.org/wiki/Liam_Neeson.

[6] Ibid.

Also Consulted:
"Liam Neeson." In *The Internet Movie Database.* Retrieved 5 November 2014 from http://www.imdb. com/name/nm0000553/.

Chapter 45: Benedict Cumberbatch

[1] "Benedict Cumberbatch." In *Wikipedia: The Free Encyclopedia.* Retrieved 9 November 2014 from http://en.wikipedia.org/wiki/Benedict_Cumberbatch.

[2] "Benedict Cumberbatch." In *The Internet Movie Database.* Retrieved 9 November 2014 from http://www.imdb.com/name/nm1212722/.

[3] Ibid.

[4] Ibid.
[5] "Benedict Cumberbatch: Inside His Surprise Wedding" by Melody Chiu. In *People*, March 2, 2015, p. 27.

Chapter 46: Jay Leno

[1] "What Drives Jay Leno?" by David Undercoffler. In *The Week*, August 1, 2014, p.36.
[2] *Leading with My Chin: Jay Leno* by Jay Leno with Bill Zehme, 1996.
[3] Ibid.
[4] "Jay Leno." In *The Internet Movie Database.* Retrieved 11 November 2014 from http://www.imdb.com/ name/ nm0005143.
[5] "What Drives Jay Leno?" by David Undercoffler. In *The Week*, August 1, 2014, p.36.
[6] Ibid.
Also Consulted:
"Jay Leno." In *Wikipedia: The Free Encyclopedia.* Retrieved 11 November 2014 from http://en.wikipedia.org/wiki/ Jay_Leno.
"Jay Leno." In *Biography.* Retrieved November 2014 from http://www.biography.com/people/jay-leno-9542191.

Summary: Patterns of Celebrity Past Lives

[1] *Children Who Remember Previous Lives: A Question of Reincarnation* by Ian Stevenson, M.D., p. 180.
[2] *Past Lives, Future Lives* by Dr. Bruce Goldberg, p. 269.
[3] *Edgar Cayce on Reincarnation* by Noel Langely, p. 84.
[4] *Many Mansions* by Gina Cerminara, p. 89.
[5] "Advances in Reincarnation Research: A Tribute to Ian Stevenson, MD." By Walter Semkiw, MD. In *IISIS: Institute for*

Integration of Science, Intuition and Spirit. Retrieved January 2015 from http://www.iisis.net/index.php?page=walter-semkiw-ian-stevenson-society-for-scientific-exploration-sse&hl=en_US.

[6] *16 Clues to Your Past Lives* by Barbara Lane, p. 132.

About the Author

Barbara Lane, Ph.D., a Clinical Hypnotherapist in private practice, was trained by some of the foremost regression therapists in the United States. In addition to *Celebrity Past-Life Clues: A Closer Look Into the Past Lives of 50 Famous People*, Dr. Lane has published several audio programs, workbooks, and other books, most notably *16 Clues to Your Past Lives: A Guide to Discovering Who You Were*.

Lane's other books on reincarnation focus on her work with the past lives of reenactors: *Echoes from the Battlefield: First-Person Accounts of Civil War Past Lives*; and *Echoes from Medieval Halls: Past-Life Memories from the Middle Ages*.

She also addressed Civil War reenactors and conducted group regressions at Gettysburg for the 135th anniversary of the battle.

Lane holds several degrees, including a Ph.D. in meta-psychology and an M.A. in metaphysics from Westbrook University, New Mexico; a B.A. in history from University of Detroit/Mercy, Michigan; and an A.A. in telecommunications from Cuesta College, California.

Since the publication of her books, Lane has become a popular guest on radio and television shows, including news and feature programs in Boston, Phoenix, Chicago and Washington D.C. She was also a guest on the Howard Stern show, during which she regressed several of his staff members on the air. Lane's work also has been featured on the *Sightings* television series and in newspapers such as the *Washington Post*, the *Philadelphia Inquirer*, the *Village Voice*.

Lane, a Michigan native, not only has worked as a reporter, anchor, producer, and director in radio and television, but also has written a metaphysical screenplay. In addition, she has worked as a crisis counselor, case manager of a homeless shelter, and a corporate trainer for the American Management Association.

An intuitive counselor, empowerment coach, and certified Reiki master, Lane combines alternative and traditional healing in her practice. She has been exposed to a wide range of alternative healing from Philippine healers and Indian gurus to Russian healing with electromagnetic energy. She has interviewed shamans in the Amazon and studied Spiritual Mind healing.

Additionally, she conducts spiritual workshops, retreats, and cruises in North and Central America on topics that range from Regressions, Soul Growth and Mission, to Utilizing the Power of the Subconscious and Healing Powers.

For over a decade, Lane was the clinical hypnotherapist on staff at the George Washington University Center for Integrative Medicine in Washington, D.C.

Her books, self-help CD's, and companion workbooks are available on Amazon, Kindle, and iTunes. You can find more information on her website: www.barbaralane.com.

Additional Books, Audio Programs, and Workbooks by
Barbara Lane, PhD.

<u>Books</u>

16 Clues to Your Past Lives: A Guide to Discovering Who You Were
Echoes from the Battlefield: First-Person Accounts of Civil War Past
Lives
Echoes from Medieval Halls: Past-Life Memories from the Middle
Ages

<u>Audio Programs</u>

Past-Life Regression: Journey Through Time Into Healing*
Enhance Test-Taking and Study Habits: Enlist Your Subconscious*
You Deserve to Be Happy: Clear the Pathway to Happiness and
Esteem*
Magnetize Career Effectiveness: Clear the Path to Career Fulfillment*
Be Fit and Trim for Life: Establish Healthy Habits for Life *
Magnetize a Lifetime Mate: Harmonize to Draw in Your Life
Partner*
The Mindbody Makeover: Look and Feel Younger and More
Radiant*
The Ultimate Mindbody Makeover: Look and Feel Younger and
More Radiant*
Want to Have a Baby: Hers: Give Yourself a Psychological and
Organic Edge*
Want to Have a Baby: His: Give Yourself a Psychological and
Organic Edge*
Create Your Life: Use Hypnosis to Make Positive Life Changes
Healthy Well-Being: Use Hypnosis to Rebalance Your Body, Mind
and Spirit

Workbooks
Past-Life Regression: Journey Through Time Into Healing Workbook
(a companion to the audio program)
*Companion workbooks also available

Books available on Amazon, Kindle and other retailers
Audio Programs available on Amazon & iTunes
Workbooks available on Amazon and Kindle

www.BarbaraLane.com